METTE N. HANDBERG

Scandinavian Christmas Stockings

First published in Great Britain in 2013
by Search Press Limited, Wellwood,
North Farm Road, Tunbridge Wells,
Kent TN2 3DR

Also published in the United States of
America in 2013 by Trafalgar Square
Books, North Pomfret, Vermont 05053

Originally published in Norwegian as
Julestrømper by Cappelen Damm AS

ISBN: 978-1-84448-944-2

Translation: Carol Huebscher Rhoades
Photography: Ragnar Hartvig
Stylist: Ingrid Skaansar
Illustrations: Mette N. Handberg
Charts: Denise Samson
Book Design: Charlotte.no

Printed in China

10 9 8 7 6 5 4 3 2 1

Publisher's note:
The author has used two traditional
Norwegian 100% wool yarns to knit the
Christmas stockings in this book (see
pages 12 and 13). If you are unable to
obtain either of these yarns, the Rauma
Gammelserie can be replaced with any
100% wool 4-ply yarn, and the Strikkegarn with a 100% wool DK yarn, though
please note the finished stockings may
vary slightly from those shown in the
book depending on the yarn used.

Contents

Foreword

I found the following in *Wikipedia*, the free online encyclopedia:

"Christmas stockings have a long tradition in Scandinavia, even earlier than when getting a visit from the Christmas elf 'in person' became customary. A long stocking or sock was hung up the evening before Christmas so that the elf, on his run through the night, could put some treats and other small items into it for the children to find when they got up on Christmas morning. After the war, it became more common for the Christmas elf to visit on Christmas Eve.

The Christmas stocking tradition has changed again, appearing during Advent and Christmas tree parties, although bags often substitute for stockings.

In the USA – where the main exchange of Christmas presents usually occurs early on Christmas morning – children hang up their Christmas stockings on Christmas Eve, either over the fireplace if there is one, at the entry to the house, or near the Christmas tree. The first thing everyone does on Christmas morning is shake out their stockings which are filled with little 'stocking stuffers' such as candy and small toys."

The first time I saw Christmas stockings was on Donald Duck. I didn't really understand why they were hung over the fireplace but it was exciting. I always wanted a really fine red Christmas stocking but I never got one. In later years, I saw many gaudy stockings made from fancy fabric, usually with printed and embossed patterns but, for me, these were completely wrong. A stocking should be knitted or it wasn't a proper stocking!

When you think about it, what can a Christmas stocking be used for today? Just for a few gifts and candies? Well, what it is used for is a matter of personal taste. It can, for example, just hang as decoration, evoking the Christmas spirit. It can be hung from the bed, over the fireplace, or in the entry hall and it can also be filled with small advent gifts, fragrant spices, or nothing.

I decided to knit my 23 Christmas stockings with Norwegian Rauma yarn. The yarn is a bit "old-fashioned" but I wanted a charming yarn with a long tradition to evoke earlier times. Of course, the stockings must be handmade! This book includes patterns for two different weights of yarn and with varying levels of knitting difficulty. Of course you can create your stocking with your own name and color choice. Before the Knitting Basics in the book you'll find three different alphabet styles to choose from if you want to knit in your own name. The little pattern motifs on each side can easily be adapted to suit your stitch count. The letters can also be changed somewhat – for example, see the "Leah" stocking where the H is narrower on the right side. You undoubtedly have some leftover yarn but choose colors carefully. Don't use colors that are too strong. Some colors belong to Christmas and you'll see them used in most of these patterns: red, black, green, gray, yellow, white, and some blue.

Some of the stockings are slightly shorter in the foot than regular socks. I have designed them so there will be more room in them for all the Advent gifts and so that small hands can reach all the way down into them.

It is not necessary to decorate the stockings; they are fine as they are. However, I have made a few suggestions for embellishments.

I am especially happy about the patterns from Selbu and West Norway. Some of the old patterns from Selbu have names that show where the inspiration was taken from, such as coffee bean, separator hook, spitball, etc.

Good luck and best wishes!

Hilsen Mette

This book is dedicated to my niece, Heidi. For several years now, she has asked me to knit her "real" Christmas stockings for her children. I had way too many ideas – so here they are!

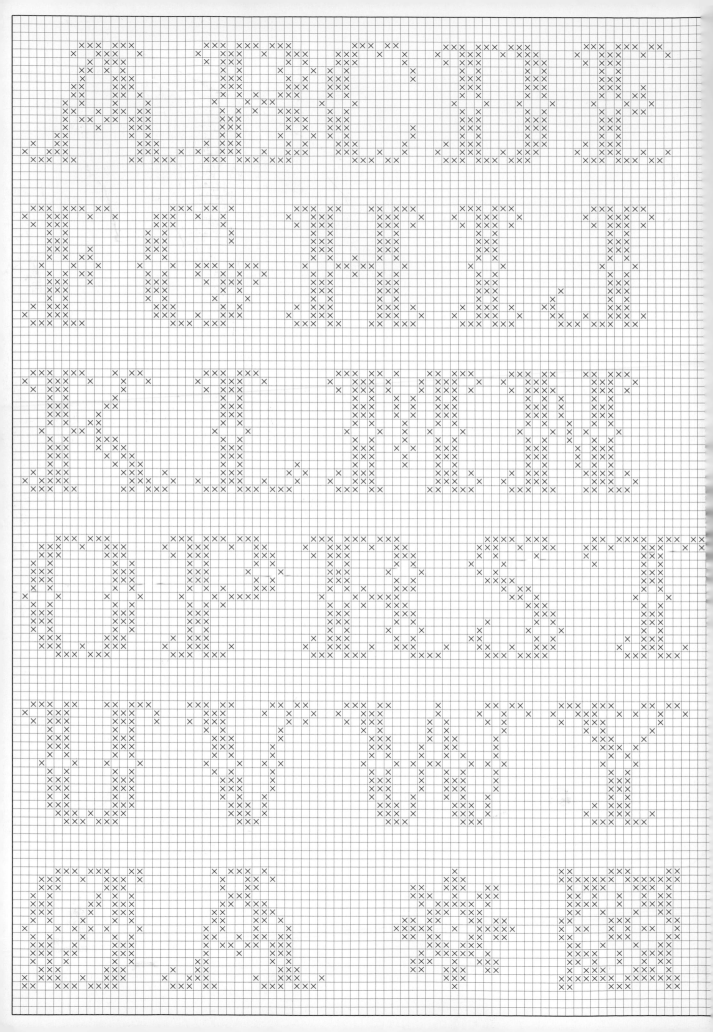

KNITTING BASICS: WHAT? HOW?

Abbreviations

BO	bind off (British cast off)
cm	centimeter(s)
CO	cast on
dpn	double pointed needle(s)
g	gram(s)
in	inch(es)
k	knit
k2tog	knit 2 together (decreases 1 stitch)
m	meter(s)
M1	make 1 = lift strand between 2 sts and knit into back loop
p	purl
rem	remain
rep	repeat
ridge	1 ridge = 2 garter st knit rows
rnd(s)	round(s)
RS	right side
sl	slip
ssk	slip, slip, knit: slip 1 knitwise, slip 1 knitwise, insert left needle into loops and knit 2 together
st(s)	stitch(es)
wyib	with yarn held in back
wyif	with yarn held in front
WS	wrong side
yd	yard(s)

Needles

Each pattern suggests needle sizes for the recommended yarn. Use the type of needles you prefer for circular knitting: a set of 4 or 5 dpn, a very short 12 in / 30 cm circular, two short circulars, or a 32 or 40 in / 80 or 100 cm long circular for Magic Loop. If you knit with a very short circular, you will also need a set of dpn for the toe. The term "needle" is used throughout and refers to whatever sort you use, whether a circular or set of dpn.

Garter Stitch Ridges

Ridges or "bead" rows result when you knit back and forth. To avoid holes when turning during knitting, you can wrap the last stitch when turning.

Knitted Cast-On (K-CO)

Make a slip knot loop, leaving a short yarn tail, and place the loop on the left needle. *Knit 1 stitch into the loop but do not drop the loop from the left needle. Slip the new stitch from the right needle back to the left needle. Repeat from * until you have the desired number of stitches.

This is an old, tried-and-true method for casting on to begin the knitted piece. It is a more elastic cast-on than the long-tail cast-on and should be used when knitting stockings. The little loops created by the knitted cast-on make it easy to pick up stitches later on.

Two-Color Stranded Knitting

Since the stockings will be used to hold presents, it is important that there not be long floats on the inside. The stockings can be hand-washed and rubbed to slightly full the surface on the inside but there is still a danger that something can catch on the yarn strands. It is best not to strand over more than 3 stitches, preferably 2, particularly at the top of the stocking, the part most subject to wear. Because some of the pattern motifs are rather large, the yarn has to be caught quite often. Make sure that you don't stack the yarn catches because the strands will be visible on the right side. If necessary, you can knit a facing for the top part of the stocking (see explanation on the next page).

Knitting Patterns with 3 Colors

Make sure that you catch the least used color on the wrong side. That twists the yarn a bit more but there aren't that many rounds with three colors in these patterns. Untwist the yarns at the end of every round. If the floats are too long, knit a facing for the top of the stocking (see page 11).

I-Cord

With dpn, cast on 3 or 4 sts. *Slide the sts back to the tip of the left needle and bring the yarn behind the stitches. Knit across the needle but *do not turn* the work. Repeat from * to desired length. Tug the yarn a bit as you work (particularly after working the first st) to keep the cord even. When the cord is complete, tug it lengthwise to further even out the stitches. You might want to practice first before you knit a cord for your stocking.

You can also make a 2-color I-cord. Knit every other row with alternating colors. Hold the yarn just used to the left, bring up the other color and knit, change color, continue as set. After the first stitch when changing colors, tighten the yarns a bit.

You can also use I-cord to edge stockings (see below).

I-Cord Edging

If you are knitting with Rauma 2-ply Gammelserie yarn, work with dpn U.S. size 2 or 3 / 3 mm or, U.S. size 4 / 3.5 mm with 3-ply Rauma Strikkegarn (use the same size needle as for pattern knitting). Make sure that you don't knit too tightly. Every now and then, pull the piece lengthwise. If the cord is too tight, begin again.

The I-cord edging can be made with either the RS or the WS facing. If you knit with the WS facing, the cord will be widest on the RS—begin by turning the stocking inside out.

With dpn, CO 4 sts. On the first row, k3, insert the left needle into the outermost loop of the stocking cast-on row, beginning at center back. Purl the last st together with the loop on the edge. Insert the needle into the next loop on the edge before you slide the sts to the left. Continue the same way until all of the cast-on edge sts have been worked. Make the I-cord about 2 in / 5 cm longer and then bind off. This last length of I-cord will provide a loop for hanging the stocking.

If you want a 2-color edging: Begin with one color and work 1 row; attach the second color. Alternate rows with the two colors. Hold the yarn just used to the left and bring the second color up around it. When joining the end of an I-cord to the beginning, graft neatly using duplicate st or Kitchener st so that the cord and hanging loop will look like a continual piece of knitting.

Knitting an Edging or Facing

Pick up the stitches directly from the cast-on row. If the edge was worked in stockinette, knit back with the same color to make the foldline. If there is a garter edge, knit around with another color. After a few rounds, make a garter foldline or an eyelet row: (k2tog, yo) around. If you are making a facing for a stocking, decrease 4 sts evenly spaced around on the 2nd rnd. The steps for knitting a facing are also described in Striped Fana (page 47) and Merry Christmas (page 38).

Facing

You can make a facing after working an I-cord edging. Use a smaller size needle, pick up and knit stitches all around the edge. After knitting 1 rnd, decrease 3 sts evenly spaced around on the next rnd. Continue knitting around until you reach a garter ridge. BO with a loose bind-off method (see below). Carefully sew down the facing all around. If you knit with 3-ply Strikkegarn, remove one of the plies so you can sew with a finer yarn. Make sure the seam doesn't pull in. You should have at least one sewn stitch into each knit stitch.

Elastic Bind-Off

*Knit 2 together, slip stitch back to the left needle and repeat from * around.

Joining with Three-Needle Bind-Off

Divide the sts which will be bound-off/ knitted together evenly onto 2 dpn. Place the needles parallel with the knit fabric RS facing RS. *Insert the right needle into the first st on the front needle without knitting it and then insert needle into the first st on the back needle. Bring the yarn over the needle and complete the stitch, knitting the 2 sts together. Repeat from * with the next st on each needle. Now there are 2 sts on the right needle. Lift the first knitted st over the second one to bind off so only 1 st remains on the right needle. Knit 2 more sts together and bind off until all the sts have been bound off. The WS of the fabric will show a little raised stripe of stitch loops. The RS should look as if it were sewn with one stitch in each stitch.

Washing

Turn the stocking inside out and hand wash it somewhat vigorously with a piece of soap in warm water. Lightly full the knitting so that the gifts won't catch on the strands floating on the inside. Do not felt the stocking completely but just enough so that the yarn floats are caught into the fabric and the stocking is a little firmer. Turn the stocking right side out and pull gently in all directions to shape and block the stocking. Leave flat to dry.

Tassels

Wind some yarn over a few fingers held together or your whole hand depending on how long you want the tassel. Remove the yarn and secure the tassel with a strand tied at the top. Let this short strand hang loose. Wrap the tassel with the desired yarn color, as wide as you like.

Pompoms

Wrap yarn around your fingers about 30 times or until the pompom is as thick as you like. Cut the yarn. Use a finer yarn to tie around all the strands, pull tight and sew back and forth so that everything is caught well. Also sew a little through the pompom so that all the strands are held in place and won't slide out. Hold the pompom by the tie strand and trim evenly around. When the pompom is nicely rounded, you can wash it. Rub it well if you want it extra firm and plump. Shake well to fluff and leave to dry. Give the pompom a last trim to make sure it is completely round.

Basic Instructions

Rauma 2-ply Gammelserie
(CYCA #2: 100% wool; 174 yd/160 m / 50 g)

This yarn is especially recommended for Christmas stockings. It is well-twisted and has a rather old-fashioned feel. The yarn is not available in a wide range of colors, but you can use leftovers of other yarns in addition to the red, black, and white. Make sure you use the same size yarn. Three-ply Strikkegarn can also be used but you need to remove one ply so that it will be the same size as the Gammelserie. This is quite easy to do. I designed the stockings with a stitch count so that you can work with a very short (12 in / 30 cm) circular instead of 4 or 5 dpn. If you are knitting with 2-ply Gammelserie yarn, needles U.S. 1-2 / 2.5 mm work well for single-color sections and needles U.S. 2-3 / 3 mm for 2-color knitting. This makes the knitting smoother and more even.

Leg
K-CO 66 sts onto a needle; join, being careful not to twist cast-on row. Place a marker at the beginning of the round and move it up each round to indicate the center back of the leg. Knit around following the chart. Continue in pattern until the piece is approx 7 in / 18 cm long or desired length. With this stitch count, you can work half of the stitches (33) for the heel with 1 center st.

Some stockings are worked somewhat differently than the Basic Instructions. This will, of course, be explained in the individual patterns.

Heel
Knit 16 sts past the center st; turn. Slip the first st purlwise wyif and then p32; turn. Slip the first st purlwise wyib, k31. Continue working back and forth in stockinette, with 1 less stitch on each row. Every time you turn, tighten the yarn a bit to avoid a hole. When there are 9 unworked sts on each side and 15 sts at the center, work 3 rounds all the way around, ending at center back. Knit the center st, k7; turn. Slip the 1st purlwise, work 14 sts; turn. Continue until all of the side sts have been worked. Continue in the round over all the sts (66) until piece measures 3¼ – 3½ in / 8 – 9 cm after the heel shaping (30 – 35 rounds).

Toe Shaping
To avoid stacking the decreases directly over each other, each decrease is shifted in relation to the previous decrease.
Decrease Rnd 1: *K4, k2tog*; repeat * to * around—55 sts rem.
Work 5 rnds without decreasing.
Decrease Rnd 2: *K2tog, k3*; rep from * to * around—44 sts rem.
Work 4 rnds without decreasing.
Decrease Rnd 3: K1, *k2tog, k2; rep from * to * around and end last rep with k1—33 sts rem.
Work 3 rnds without decreasing.
Decrease Rnd 4: *K1, k2tog*; rep from * to * around—22 sts rem.
Work 2 rnds without decreasing.
Finishing: K2tog around and then knit 1 more rnd. Cut yarn and pull end through remaining 11 sts.

3-ply Strikkegarn

(CYCA #3: 100% wool; 114 yd/105 m / 50 g)

The stitch count for stockings knit with 3-ply Strikkegarn makes it possible to work on a 12 in / 30 cm circular rather than 4 or 5 dpn. Usually this yarn is knit with US. size 4 / 3.5 mm needles but we recommend using U.S. size 2-3 / 3 mm for single-colored areas and U.S. 4 / 3.5 mm for 2-color knitting. Some of the patterns differ a little from the Basic Instructions given here. The differences are, of course, explained in the individual patterns.

Leg

K-CO 60 sts onto a needle; join, being careful not to twist cast-on row. Place a marker at the beginning of the round and move it up each round to indicate the center back of the leg. Knit around following the chart. Continue in pattern until the piece is approx 7 in / 18 cm long or desired length. With this stitch count, you can work half of the stitches (30) for the heel with 2 center sts.

Heel

Knit 15 sts past the center st; turn. Slip the first st purlwise wyif and then p29; turn. Slip the first st purlwise wyib, k28. Continue working back and forth in stockinette, with 1 less stitch on each row. Every time you turn, tighten the yarn a bit to avoid a hole. When there are 8 unworked sts on each side and 14 sts at the center, work 3 rounds all the way around, ending at center back. Knit the center st, k7; turn. Slip the 1st purlwise, work 13 sts; turn. Continue until all of the side sts have been worked. Continue in the round over all the sts (60) until piece measures 3¼ – 3½ in / 8 – 9 cm after the heel shaping (20 – 25 rounds).

Toe Shaping

To avoid stacking the decreases directly over each other, each decrease is shifted in relation to the previous decrease.

Decrease Rnd 1: *K4, k2tog*; repeat * to * around—50 sts rem.

Work 5 rnds without decreasing.

Decrease Rnd 2: *K2tog, k3*; rep from * to * around—40 sts rem.

Work 4 rnds without decreasing.

Decrease Rnd 3: K1, *k2tog, k2; rep from * to * around and end last rep with k1—30 sts rem.

Work 3 rnds without decreasing.

Decrease Rnd 4: *K1, k2tog*; rep from * to * around—20 sts rem.

Work 2 rnds without decreasing.

Finishing: K2tog around and then knit 1 more rnd. Cut yarn and pull end through remaining 10 sts.

Leah
Dance around the Christmas Tree

Before you begin knitting, read the Basic Instructions for 2-ply Gammel-serie yarn (page 12), and Two-Color Stranded Knitting (page 10), paying particular attention to the advice about catching the floats on the wrong side. This design has one 3-color round.

Yarn
Rauma 2-ply Gammelserie, 1 ball each: red 424, brown-black 410, white 401; 3-ply Strikkegarn: yellow 131 (Remove 1 ply of the Strikkegarn before knitting. The remaining 2 plies will make the yarn the same size as the Gammelserie yarn; otherwise use a small amount of 2-ply yarn).

Needles
U.S. sizes 1-2 and 2-3 / 2.5 and 3 mm

Instructions
With larger size needle and red, K-CO 66 sts (see page 10). Working back and forth, knit 3 rows. Change to black and knit 2 rows. This makes a total of 3 ridges. Join to work in the round, and follow the charted pattern on page 16. After completing charted rows, change to smaller size needle and knit 5 rounds.

Heel
Follow the Basic Instructions for the heel on page 12.
After the heel, knit around for 3½ – 4 in / 9 – 10 cm or about 30-35 rnds.

Toe
Follow the Basic Instructions for the toe on page 12.

Finishing
Weave in all ends securely on WS except for the cast-on tail. With larger needle and black and red yarn, make a 2-color I-Cord edging along the top of the stocking. Graft end of hanging loop to beginning of I-cord edging. Weave in remaining ends. Wash and block the stocking (see page 11). Make a small pompom with red and black yarn. Trim the pompom as round as possible, wash and shake to fluff. When the pompom is dry, trim evenly. Attach at base of the hanging loop.

◀ LEAH

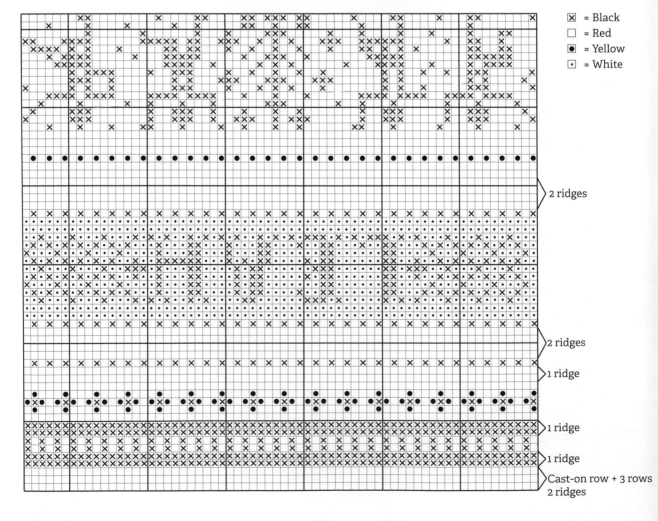

☒ = Black
☐ = Red
⊙ = Yellow
⊡ = White

2 ridges

2 ridges

1 ridge

1 ridge

1 ridge

Cast-on row + 3 rows

2 ridges

16

BLACK CATS ▶

⊠ = Black
☐ = Red
⊙ = Green
⊡ = White

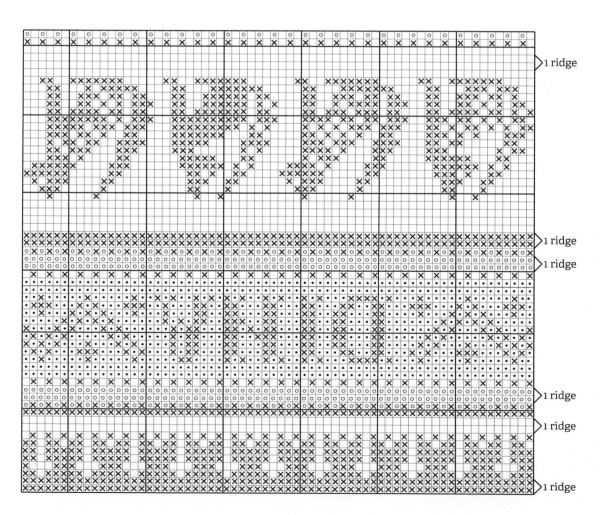

Black Cats
Animal Motifs from Selbu

Before you begin knitting, read the Basic Instructions for 2-ply Gammel-serie yarn (page 12), and Two-Color Stranded Knitting (page 10), paying particular attention to the advice about catching the floats on the wrong side. There are some rather long floats in this design.

Yarn
Rauma 2-ply Gammelserie, 1 ball each: red 424, brown-black 410, white 401; 3-ply Strikkegarn: green 145 (remove 1 ply of the Strikkegarn before knitting; the remaining 2 plies will make the yarn the same size as the Gammelserie yarn)

Needles
U.S. sizes 1-2 and 2-3 / 2.5 and 3 mm

Instructions
With larger size needle and black, K-CO 66 sts (see page 10). Turn and knit 1 row. Turn, join to work in the round (the RS is now facing), and follow the charted pattern on page 17. After completing charted rows, change to smaller needle and knit 3 rounds with red.

Heel
Follow the Basic Instructions for the heel on page 12.
After the heel, knit around for 3½ – 4 in / 9 – 10 cm or about 30-33 rnds.

Toe
After the first decrease round, work a pattern motif (see small chart on page 17) in the rnds without decreasing. Begin with: *K1 with black, k4 with red; rep from * around. On the 2nd decrease rnd, the decreases will fall between the small crosses. After the decrease rnd, work the round with black "dots." Continue to end of toe shaping.

Finishing
Weave in all ends securely on WS except for the cast-on tail. With larger needle and green, make an I-Cord edging along the top of the stocking and then a hanging loop (see page 10). Graft the hanging loop to the beginning of I-cord edging. Weave in remaining ends. Wash and block the stocking (see page 11).
Make a long tassel (see page 11) with red or red and black. Twist black yarn around the tassel to secure and decorate. Carefully wash the tassel and shake it to fluff. Attach to the toe securely with duplicate stitch (see photo).

Folk Dance

Before you begin knitting, read the Basic Instructions for 2-ply Gammelserie yarn (page 12), and Two-Color Stranded Knitting (page 10), paying particular attention to the advice about catching the floats on the wrong side. This design has one 3-color round.

Yarn
Rauma 2-ply Gammelserie, 1 ball each: red 424, brown-black 410, white 401; 3-ply Strikkegarn: dark red 128 and yellow 131 (Remove 1 ply of the Strikkegarn before knitting. The remaining 2 plies will make the yarn the same size as the Gammelserie yarn; otherwise use a small amount of 2-ply yarn).

Needles
U.S. sizes 1-2 and 2-3 / 2.5 and 3 mm

Instructions
With larger size needle and red, K-CO 64 sts (see page 10). **Note**: the smaller cast-on number is adjusted for the pattern repeats). Turn and knit 1 row. Turn, join to work in the round (the RS is now facing), and follow the charted pattern on page 22. After completing charted rows, change to smaller needle and knit 4 rounds with red.

Heel
Follow the Basic Instructions for the heel (see page 12) but work with 32 sts. There will be 9 unworked sts on each side and 14 sts at the center. After the heel, knit around for about 30-35 rnds.

Toe
Because of the stitch count, the standard toe shaping has been adjusted as follows (try not to stack decreases).
Decrease Rnd 1: *K6, k2tog*; rep from * to * around – 56 sts remain.
Knit 5 rnds without decreasing.
Decrease Rnd 2: *K5, k2tog*; rep from * to * around – 48 sts remain.
Knit 4 rnds without decreasing.
Decrease Rnd 3: *K4, k2tog*; rep from * to * around – 40 sts remain.
Knit 3 rnds without decreasing.
Decrease Rnd 4: *K3, k2tog*; rep from * to * around – 32 sts remain.
Add in dark red and work *k1 dark red, k3 red*; rep * to * around. On the next rnd, work k2 dark red, *k1 red, k3 dark red*; rep * to * around and end with k1 dark red. Cut red and continue with dark red only.
Next decrease rnd: *K2, k2tog*; rep * to * around (the decreases should fall between the points of the color change) – 24 sts remain.
Knit 1 rnd without decreasing.
Next: *K1, k2tog*; rep * to * around – 16 sts remain.
Knit 1 rnd without decreasing.

◄ FOLK DANCE

K2tog around and then knit 1 more round without decreasing. Cut yarn and draw end through remaining 8 sts.

Finishing

Weave in all ends securely on WS except for the cast-on tail. With larger needle and black, make an I-Cord edging along the top of the stocking and then a hanging loop (see page 10). Graft the hanging loop to beginning of I-cord edging.

Weave in remaining ends. Wash and block the stocking (see page 11). Make a little tassel (see page 11) for the toe. For this tassel, crochet the cord directly from the yarn in the tassel. Lightly wash the tassel so it will hang more smoothly. Attach tassel.

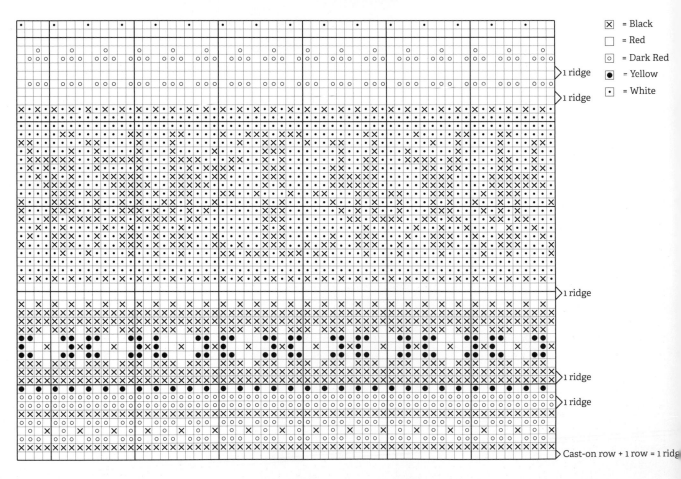

☒ = Black
☐ = Red
⊙ = Dark Red
● = Yellow
• = White

CHRISTMAS ▶

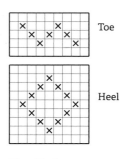

Toe

Heel

⊠ = Black

☐ = Red

⊡ = Gray

⊡ = White

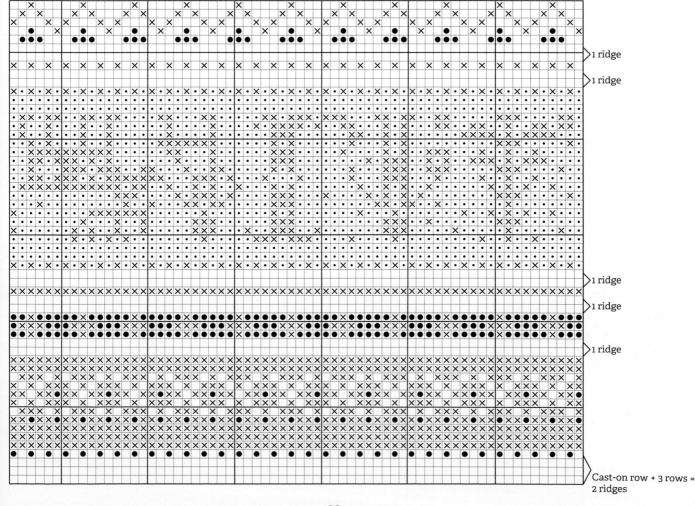

1 ridge

1 ridge

1 ridge

1 ridge

1 ridge

Cast-on row + 3 rows =
2 ridges

Christmas

Before you begin knitting, read the Basic Instructions for 2-ply Gammelserie yarn (page 12), and Two-Color Stranded Knitting (page 10), paying particular attention to the advice about catching the floats on the wrong side. This design has two 3-color rounds.

Yarn

Rauma 2-ply Gammelserie, 1 ball each: red 424, brown-black 410, white 401, gray 405

Needles

U.S. sizes 1-2 and 2-3 / 2.5 and 3 mm

Instructions

With larger size needle and red, K-CO 66 sts (see page 10). Working back and forth, knit 3 rows. Join to work in the round (the RS is now facing) and follow the charted pattern on page 23. After completing charted rows, change to smaller needle and knit 1 rnd with red. Next rnd: Knit around with 1 purl between each of the black points. Knit another 4 – 5 rnds.

Heel

Follow the basic heel instructions (page 12) for approx 8 rows. Now, on the RS, add in a strand of black yarn about 15¾ in / 40 cm long and knit the st at the center back with the center of the black strand; complete row as set. On the next, WS row, use each side of the black strand to work the 2 sts of the block pattern (see Heel chart on page 23). Continue the heel following the Basic Instructions and then knit about 30 – 35 rounds for the foot or to desired length.

Toe

Shape the toe as described in the Basic Instructions (page 12) but make a little zigzag motif after the second decrease rnd (see chart, page 23) + 1 rnd. Continue with red.

Finishing

Weave in all ends securely on WS except for the cast-on tail. With larger needle and gray and black yarn, K-CO 4 sts and make a 2-color I-Cord edging along the top of the stocking and then a hanging loop (see page 10). Graft the hanging loop to beginning of I-cord edging. Weave in remaining ends. Wash and block the stocking (see page 11).

Make a small gray tassel (see page 11) to attach near the hanging loop. This one is wrapped with red yarn embellished with little black dots. Lightly wash the tassel so it will hang more smoothly. Attach tassel. Trim the red and black yarns so they will be part of the tassel. Wrap the end of the yarn used to attach the tassel very tightly, folding the yarn around the tassel. That will make it twist automatically. Attach the yarn at that point. Carefully wash the tassel and shake it out. The cord is attached to the stocking with a button made of an old Norwegian 1-øring coin. You could also use an old pewter button, perhaps with an animal motif.

Henrik

Before you begin knitting, read the Basic Instructions for 2-ply Gammelserie yarn (page 12), and Two-Color Stranded Knitting (page 10), paying particular attention to the advice about catching the floats on the wrong side.

Yarn
Rauma 2-ply Gammelserie, 1 ball each: red 424, brown-black 410, blue 438, white 400 or 401

Needles
U.S. sizes 1-2 and 2-3 / 2.5 and 3 mm

Instructions
With larger size needle and red, K-CO 66 sts (see cast-on instructions, page 10). Knit 1 row; turn and join to work in the round (RS is now facing). Follow the charted pattern on page 28. After completing charted rows, change to smaller needle and knit approx 5 rounds with red only. Complete the stocking following the Basic Instructions for Gammelserie yarn (page 12).

Finishing
Weave in all ends securely on WS except for the cast-on tail. With blue, K-CO 4 sts and make an I-Cord edging along the top of the stocking finishing with a hanging loop. Graft the hanging loop to beginning of I-cord edging. Weave in remaining ends. Wash and block the stocking (see page 11).

◄ HENRIK

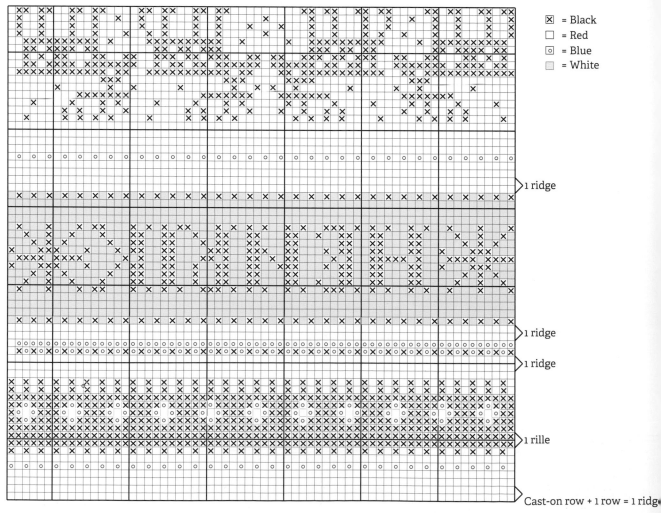

☒ = Black
☐ = Red
⊡ = Blue
▨ = White

1 ridge

1 ridge

1 ridge

1 rille

Cast-on row + 1 row = 1 ridge

MAILIN ▶

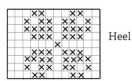

Heel

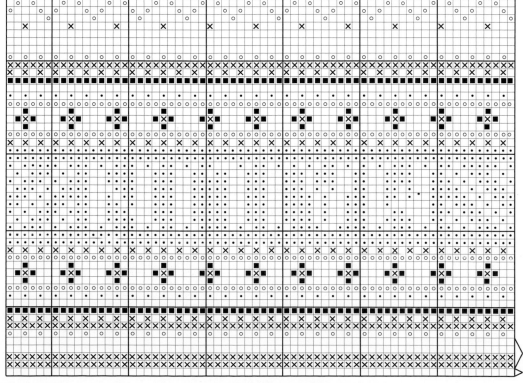

□ = Red
☒ = Black
⊙ = Gray
■ = Yellow
⊡ = White

2 ridges

Cast-on row + 1 row = 1 ridge

Mailin

Before you begin knitting, read the Basic Instructions for 2-ply Gammel-serie yarn (page 12), and Two-Color Stranded Knitting (page 10), paying particular attention to the advice about catching the floats on the wrong side. This design has two 3-color rounds.

Yarn
Rauma 2-ply Gammelserie, 1 ball each: red 424, brown-black 410, gray 405, white 400 or 401; 3-ply Strikkegarn: yellow 131 (Remove 1 ply of the Strik-kegarn before knitting. The remaining 2 plies will make the yarn the same size as the Gammelserie yarn; otherwise use a small amount of 2-ply yarn).

Needles
U.S. sizes 1-2 and 2-3 / 2.5 and 3 mm

Instructions
With larger size needle and red, K-CO 66 sts (see cast-on instructions, page 10). Do not join. Working back and forth, knit 1 row; add black and knit 2 rows with black followed by 2 knit rows with red. This makes a total of 3 ridges on the RS. Join to work in the round and follow the charted pattern on page 29. After completing charted rows, change to smaller size needle and knit approx 8 rounds with red.

Heel
Follow the Basic Instructions for the heel on page 12. *At the same time as beginning heel,* attach a long strand of black, with the center of the strand at center back of the stocking. Work the heel chart on page 29, working back and forth in stockinette. Shape heel until there are 2 unworked sts on each side. Complete heel and work foot as for the Basic Instructions.

Toe
Follow the Basic Instructions for the toe on page 12.

Finishing
Weave in all ends securely on WS except for the cast-on tail. With larger needle and black, K-CO 4 and make an I-Cord edging along the top of the stocking. Graft the hanging loop to beginning of I-cord edging. Weave in remaining ends. Wash and block the stocking (see page 11).
A little gray tassel is attached to the toe. It is wrapped with red yarn deco-rated with small yellow dots (see photo). Wrap the yarn at the top of the tassel very tightly, fold it back towards the tassel and secure the end. Hide the red and yellow yarn ends in the tassel. Wash the tassel carefully and shake it out. See photo.

Hearts

Before you begin knitting, read the Basic Instructions for 2-ply Gammel-serie yarn (page 12), and Two-Color Stranded Knitting (page 10), paying particular attention to the advice about catching the floats on the wrong side.

Yarn

Rauma 2-ply Gammelserie, 1 ball each: red 424, brown-black 410, white 401; 3-ply Strikkegarn: yellow 131 (remove 1 ply of the Strikkegarn before knitting; the remaining 2 plies will make the yarn the same size as the Gammelserie yarn)

Needles

U.S. sizes 1-2 and 2-3 / 2.5 and 3 mm

Instructions

With larger size needle and red, K-CO 66 sts (see page 10). Join to work in the round, being careful not to twist cast-on sts. Work following the chart on page 34. After completing charted rows, change to smaller needle and continue with red only for 1¼ – 1½ in / 3 – 4 cm.

Heel

Follow the Basic Instructions for the heel on page 12.
After the heel, knit around for 1½ in / 3.5 cm. Knit 1 rnd, alternating black and yellow; knit 4 rnds red and then another rnd alternating black and yellow. Continue with red only for approx 1½ in / 3.5 cm.

Toe

Follow the Basic Instructions for the toe on page 12.

Finishing

Weave in all ends securely on WS except for the cast-on tail. With larger needle, and yellow and black yarn, K-CO 4 sts and make a 2-color I-Cord edging along the top of the stocking. For this stocking, the I-cord is also used for attaching the tassels. Work the I-cord for a couple of inches / approx 5 cm before beginning the edging and for the same amount after the edging. Graft the hanging loop to I-cord edging. Weave in remaining ends. Wash and block the stocking (see page 11).
The tassels hanging on the I-cord should be a bit heavier than usual. Make 2 tassels – one yellow, one black. Wrap each tassel with the opposite color, yellow on black and black on yellow. On the stocking shown here, the tassels are also embellished with dots and dashes (see photo).
Wash the tassels lightly and shake out well so they will hang more smoothly (see photo).

◄ HEARTS

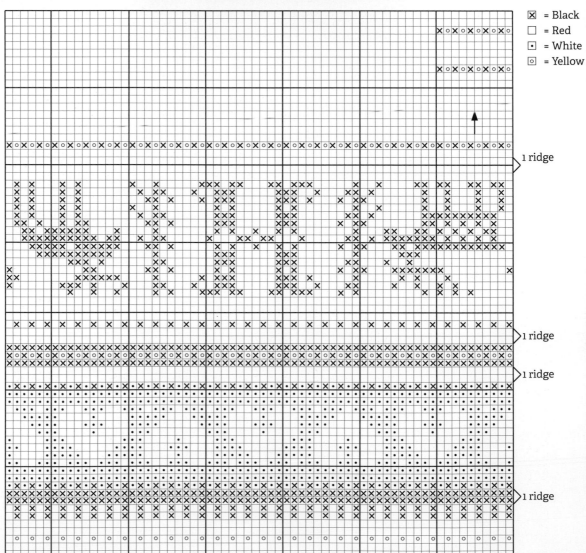

MERRY CHRISTMAS ▶

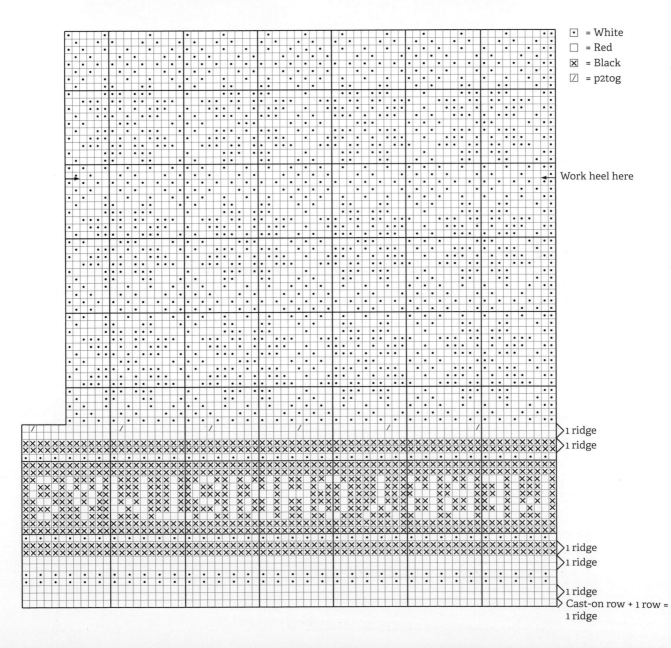

⊡ = White

☐ = Red

☒ = Black

⧄ = p2tog

Work heel here

1 ridge
1 ridge

1 ridge
1 ridge

1 ridge
Cast-on row + 1 row =
1 ridge

Merry Christmas

Selbu "Endless Rose"

Before you begin knitting, read the Basic Instructions for 2-ply Gammelserie yarn (page 12), and Two-Color Stranded Knitting (page 10), paying particular attention to the advice about catching the floats on the wrong side. The stocking shown here has two repeats of the pattern before the heel. It is rather long so you can work only one pattern repeat if you prefer. You can also knit a few more single-color rounds before the toe.

Yarn

Rauma 2-ply Gammelserie, 1 ball each: red 424, white 401, brown-black 410

Needles

U.S. sizes 1-2 and 2-3 / 2.5 and 3 mm

Instructions

With larger size needle and red, K-CO 72 sts (see page 10). Working back and forth, knit 3 rows. Join and work in the round following the chart on page 35.

Note: Decrease to 70 sts on the 5th rnd after the wording (on the purl rnd of the black ridge) and to 66 on the 7th rnd after the wording (purl rnd of the red ridge). Work the "rose" (star) pattern until you've completed 2 repeats. The white stripe down the center back begins at the top and continues to the toe. Begin the pattern at this center stitch.

Heel

The heel for this stocking differs somewhat from the basic heel described on page 12 (see arrow at side of chart for heel placement). First, work 31 sts with 15 sts on each side of the center st. Continue (working in check pattern) the heel as explained in the Basic Instructions until 8 unworked sts remain on each side with 15 sts at the center.

On the next row, work over all the heel sts and continue until 16 sts have been worked (= 1 extra st); turn and do the same on the other side. The sts in some areas may be the same color as the previous st but it doesn't matter. Complete the heel and then continue in pattern for 1 or 2 repeats on the foot. Note that, just before the toe, some small crosses are added to the pattern (see chart). Cut white.

Toe

Change to smaller needle and knit 1 rnd with red. Continue, following the Basic Instructions (see page 12). This model has the toe decreased all the way down to 4 sts and then a few rows of I-cord to make a little tip.

After completing rnds for the basic toe, work as follows:

(K2tog) 5 times, k1 – 6 sts remain.

Knit 1 rnd.

(K1, k2tog) 2 times – 4 sts remain.

Work a 5-row I-cord over the remaining 4 sts.

BO and sew end of cord to tip of toe.

Finishing

Weave in all ends securely on WS except for the cast-on tail. If there are any small openings along the heel shaping, stitch them closed. Turn the stocking inside out and knit a 3-stitch I-cord edging at the top with white and larger needle. Graft the ends of the I-cord and weave in remaining ends. With WS of edging facing, pick up and knit 3 sts, about ¾ in / 2 cm to the side of the center and make an I-cord about 2 in / 5 cm long. Shape the cord into a loop over the center back and stitch it down (see photo). Wash and block the stocking (see page 11).

Happy Holidays

Selbu "Endless Rose" with snowflakes and roses

Before you begin knitting, read the Basic Instructions for 2-ply Gammelserie yarn (page 12), and Two-Color Stranded Knitting (page 10), paying particular attention to the advice about catching the floats on the wrong side.

Yarn

Rauma 2-ply Gammelserie, 1 ball each: dark blue 447, red 424, white 401

Needles

U.S. sizes 1-2 and 2-3 / 2.5 and 3 mm

Instructions

With larger size needle and blue, K-CO 66 sts (see page 10). Knit 1 row; turn so the RS is now facing. Join and work in the round following the chart on page 41. **Note:** that you decrease to 64 sts total in the white round before the hearts and increase back to 66 sts on the second white round after completing the hearts. Continue in pattern until you reach the marker for the heel; cut yarns.

Heel

The heel for this stocking differs somewhat from the basic heel described on page 12. Work the heel with smaller needle and red over only 31 sts at center back. Continue until there are 8 unworked sts on each side and 15 sts at the center. On the next row, work over all the heel sts and continue over the unworked sts + 1 st; turn. Sl 1 and work over the sts on the other side the same way; turn. Continue with the heel as in the Basic Instructions (see page 12) until 1 st with red remains. Do the same on the other side, ending at center back. Cut red and change back to blue and white and larger needle. Continue in pattern until you've worked a total of 3 whole diamonds down center front. Cut yarns. Attach red and and knit 1 rnd.

Toe

Change to smaller needle and work toe following Basic Instructions (see page 12).

Finishing

Weave in all ends securely on WS except for the cast-on tail. With smaller needle, pick up 66 sts around the cast-on edge. Make sure you pick up the same number of sts as cast-on (it's easy to end up with 1 st less).

Knit 2 rnds with red. Make an eyelet round: *yo, k2tog*; rep * to * around. Continue with red and knit 2 rnds. On the next rnd, decrease 4 sts evenly spaced around: (K14, k2tog, k15, k2tog) 2 times. This makes the facing a bit tighter for a good fit inside the stocking. Knit around on the facing for approx 24 rnds or until facing covers the heart panel down to red garter ridge. BO loosely (see page 11).

Sew down the facing at the red ridge with 1 sewn st into each knit st. It's important that the facing not pull in. For the hanging loop, pick up 3 or 4 sts in one of the small points of the eyelet foldline a little to the side of the center back and knit an I-cord about 2 in / 5 cm long. Fold the cord so it is flat and sew down on the other side of center back. Wash and block the stocking (see page 11). Occasionally pat facing smooth as the stocking dries.

◄ HAPPY HOLIDAYS

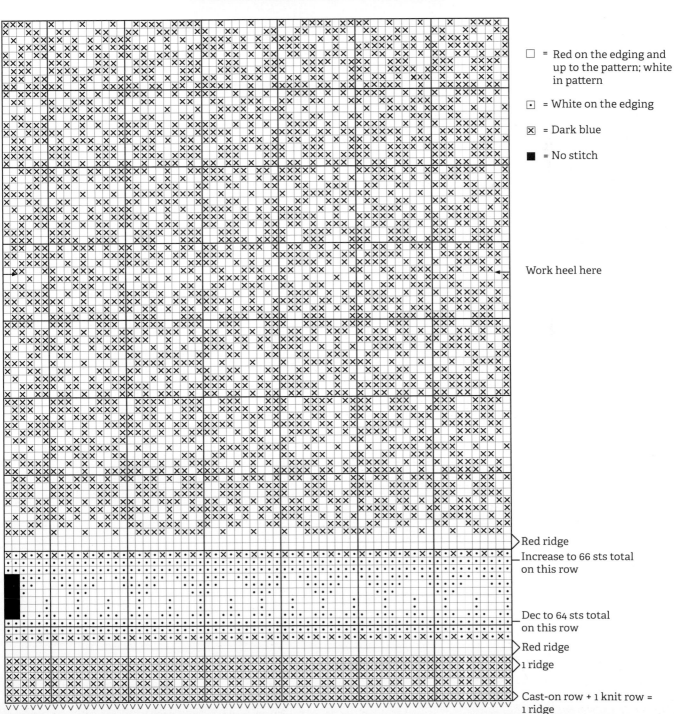

□ = Red on the edging and
    up to the pattern; white
    in pattern

⊡ = White on the edging

☒ = Dark blue

■ = No stitch

Work heel here

Red ridge

Increase to 66 sts total
on this row

Dec to 64 sts total
on this row

Red ridge

1 ridge

Cast-on row + 1 knit row =
1 ridge

Snowman

Before you begin knitting, read the Basic Instructions for 2-ply Gammelserie yarn (page 12), and Two-Color Stranded Knitting (page 10), paying particular attention to the advice about catching the floats on the wrong side. This design has many rounds with long floats. This stocking has a rather short foot after the heel. There is 1 round with 3 colors.

Yarn
Rauma 2-ply Gammelserie, 1 ball each: dark blue 447, blue 438, red 424, white 400

Needles
U.S. sizes 1-2 and 2-3 / 2.5 and 3 mm

Instructions
With larger size needle and dark blue, K-CO 66 sts (see page 10). Knit 1 row; turn so the RS is now facing. Join and work in the round following the chart on page 44. After completing charted motifs, change to smaller needle and continue in stripe pattern. Work the heel after you've completed the third light blue stripe.

Heel
Finish with the light blue stripe. Work the heel following the Basic Instructions on page 12. (Optional) On the 4th row (knit) begin the text: GOD JUL with red. The "O" should be at the center back so count the sts for the letters from that point. Continue as for the basic heel.

Foot and Toe
The foot begins with 3 rnds of dark blue. After that, work 7 – 8 stripes or as many as desired and then knit 1 rnd with the next color. Now shape the toe as for the Basic Instructions (see page 12), working in stripes to the end of the toe.

Finishing
Weave in all ends securely on WS except for the cast-on tail. Turn the stocking inside out and, with larger needle and red, K-CO 4 sts. Work an I-cord for the edging and hanging loop. Graft the hanging loop to beginning of I-cord edging. Weave in remaining ends. Wash and block the stocking (see page 11).

I decorated this stocking with 5 white pom-pom "snowballs" (see the section on small round pompoms on page 11). Cut yarn to make a twisted cord about 1.5 yd / m long. Twist the cord, holding one end with your right hand. Pull out a piece about 8 in / 20 cm and let the yarn twist on itself. Pinch at that point and pull out another short piece to make another little cord. You can make as many cords as you want in slightly varying lengths. Bind them together to finish. Make as many small pompoms as you have cords.

Trim the pompoms as round and even as possible. Wash them well; shake them out and leave to dry. They should be as plump as possible. When they are dry, trim them into their final shape. Sew a tassel onto each end. Sew on a pewter button (preferably one with a snowflake motif) to hold everything together. You might need to bend the button slightly to hide the ends of the cords. See photo.

◄ SNOWMAN

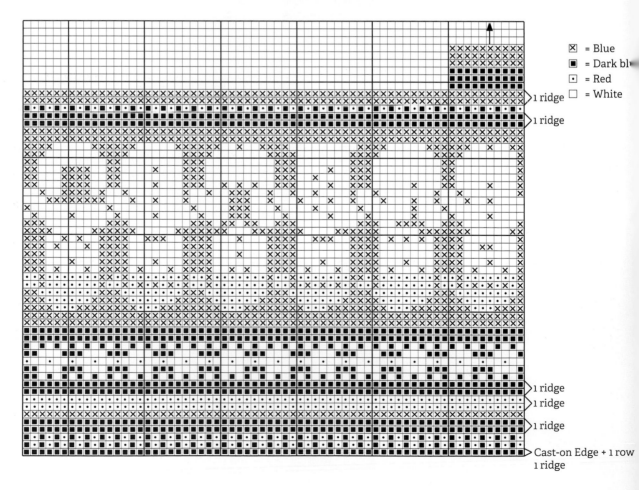

1 ridge

1 ridge

1 ridge

1 ridge

1 ridge

Cast-on Edge + 1 row
1 ridge

☒ = Blue
■ = Dark bl
⊡ = Red
☐ = White

44

STRIPED FANA ▶

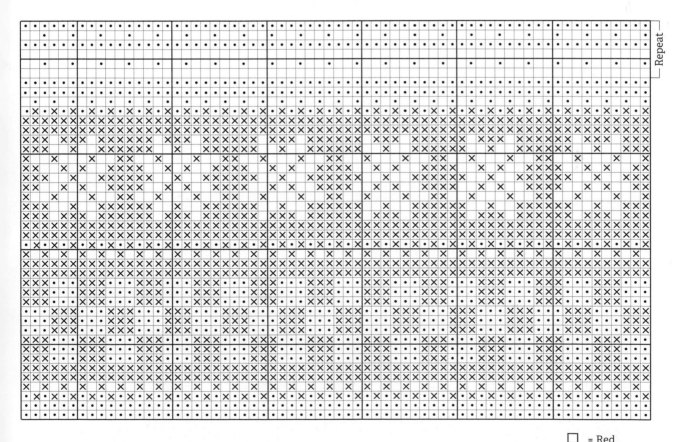

Repeat

☐ = Red

☒ = Black

⊡ = Gray

Striped Fana

Inspired by the "striped sweaters" from Fana in Hordaland province, Norway

Before you begin knitting, read the Basic Instructions for 2-ply Gammelserie yarn (page 12), and Two-Color Stranded Knitting (page 10), paying particular attention to the advice about catching the floats on the wrong side.

Yarn

Rauma 2-ply Gammelserie, 1 ball each: brown-black 410, gray 405, red 424

Needles

U.S. sizes 1-2 and 2-3 / 2.5 and 3 mm

Instructions

With larger size needle and gray, K-CO 66 sts (see page 10). Join, being careful not to twist cast-on row. Work charted pattern on page 45. After the block and star patterns, continue in charted stripe pattern repeat until there are 3 gray stripes. Work heel beginning on second rnd of a red stripe.

Heel

The heel is worked entirely with red (use smaller size needle). Follow the Basic Instructions for the heel on page 12. When the first half of the heel is complete, work around on all the sts with red and then work the second half of the heel. Work the foot in stripe pattern as set until there are 5 gray stripes and 5 red stripes; the last stripe is red.

Toe

Shape the toe as described in the Basic Instructions (page 12).

Finishing

Weave in all ends securely on WS except for the cast-on tail. With gray and smaller needle, pick up and knit sts along the cast-on row and purl back (purl on the RS) for the foldline so the facing won't show on the RS. Change to red and knit 2 rnds. On the next rnd, decrease 4 sts evenly spaced around. Knit around for the facing until it covers the black/gray blocks.
BO loosely (see page 11). Sew down the facing with one sewn stitch into each knit stitch. At the top of the red facing, pick up and knit 3 or 4 sts and make an I-cord (see page 10). This loop can lie flat against the stocking (see picture). Attach the loop and weave in remaining ends. Wash and block the stocking (see page 11). If you like, make and attach a small red tassel or pompom at the toe.

Single-Color Fana

Inspired by the men's "white sweaters" from Fana in Hordaland province, Norway.

Before you begin knitting, read the Basic Instructions for 2-ply Gammelserie yarn (page 12), and Two-Color Stranded Knitting (page 10), paying particular attention to the advice about catching the floats on the wrong side.

Yarn
Rauma 2-ply Gammelserie, 1 ball each: white 401, red 424, brown-black 410 or gray 405

Needles
U.S. sizes 1-2 and 2-3 / 2.5 and 3 mm

Instructions
With smaller size needle and black or gray, K-CO 66 sts (see page 10). Cut yarn and attach white. Working back and forth, knit 4 rows; the last row is knit on the WS. Join and continue in the round. All of the sts that are purled on the RS are marked as pattern sts on the chart (see next page). Instead of purl rounds on the RS, yo, turn the work and knit back (see page 50). On the next round, knit the yarnover with the following stitch to avoid a hole at the turn. The pattern on the front of the stocking can be omitted or worked following the chart. Begin the heel shaping after the second diamond on the front or after approx 2 in / 5 cm.

Heel
(Optional) with red, work in GOD JUL on the heel. Begin on the RS after the first heel shaping row on each side. Continue as explained in the Basic Instructions (page 12), working the heel over 32 sts.

Foot and Toe
Work the foot, continuing charted pattern, until foot is approx 3¼ – 3½ in / 8 – 9 cm after the heel shaping (30 – 35 rounds). For this stocking, the decreases for the toe are stacked one above the other and the decreases are worked with p2tog: 1st decrease rnd: K4, p2tog. Next decrease rnd: K3, p2tog. Continue as set.

Finishing
Turn stocking inside out so that the I-cord is worked from the WS. Make a 2-color I-cord and hanging loop with red and white: K-CO 4 sts and work I-cord. Graft the hanging loop to the beginning of the I-cord, using both

SINGLE-COLOR FANA

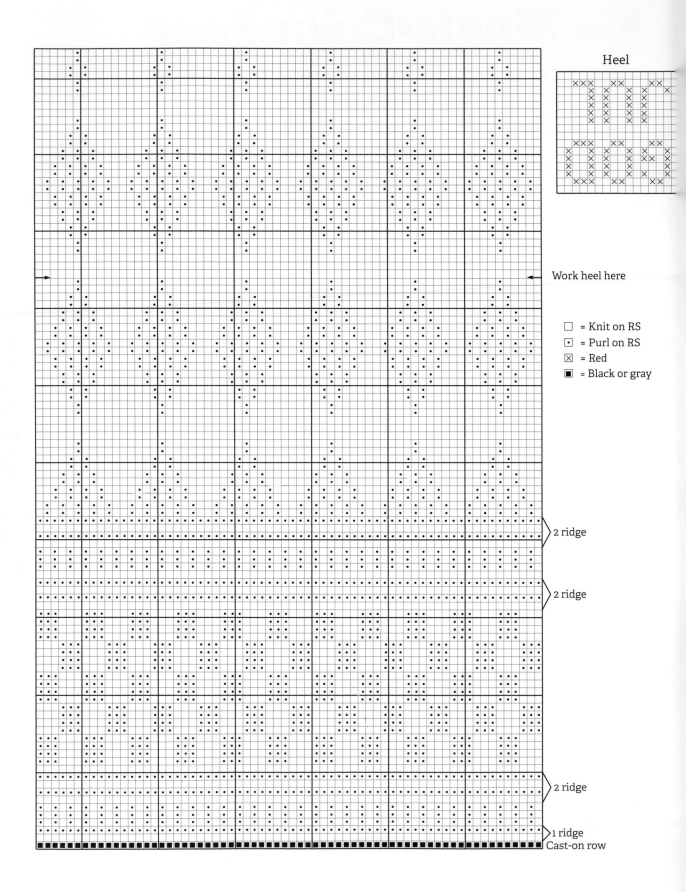

Heel

Work heel here

☐ = Knit on RS
⊡ = Purl on RS
☒ = Red
■ = Black or gray

2 ridge

2 ridge

2 ridge

1 ridge
Cast-on row

colors so the knitting looks continuous. Wash and block stocking (see page 11). Weave in all ends securely on the WS.

Embellish the hanging loop with 2 small tassels. Make a small cord with 1 red and 1 white strand. Twist the yarn so it doesn't knot at the ends which will be sewn securely to the tassels (see explanation for the Snow-men pattern, page 42). Wrap the small red tassel with black and white and make a slightly larger black tassel wrapped with red and white.

The knot on the cord is covered with a small button. In the old days, silver coins were used as buttons, particularly on fine clothes. The button shown here is a Norwegian 10-øring coin with a hole but you can also use a pewter button with a rosette pattern.

Mom + Dad

With the two hearts as one motif from Selbu on the back.

Before you begin knitting, read the Basic Instructions for 2-ply Gammelserie yarn (page 12), and Two-Color Stranded Knitting (page 10), paying particular attention to the advice about catching the floats on the wrong side. This design has long floats throughout the heart motif on the front.

Yarn
Rauma 2-ply Gammelserie, 1 ball each: red 424, brown-black 410

Needles
U.S. sizes 1-2 and 2-3 / 2.5 and 3 mm

Notions: 2 small pewter buttons for embellishment

Instructions
With larger size needle and red, K-CO 96 sts (see page 10) and join, being careful not to twist cast-on row. Work following the chart on page 54 and then knit 1 rnd in red.

Heels
Change to smaller size needle. This stocking is worked with a short row "heel" (see page 12) centered over each of the large motifs. First, knit to the center st of the large heart motif on stocking front. Knit the center st + 15 more sts; turn. Sl 1 purlwise, p30 (= 31 sts total); turn and knit until 1 st remains; turn and continue as for basic heel instructions.
At the same time, on Row 5 of the heel, cut a length of black about 20 in / 51 cm long and use to work the small heart (see chart on page 54 and work heart with intarsia technique) at the center of the heel. If you prefer, you can, instead, embroider the hearts on the front and

back of the "heel" afterwards using duplicate stitch.
Work heel until 3 sts remain at the tip (14 sts remain at each side of the center 3 sts) and then work 5 rows back and forth over these 3 sts; cut yarn, leaving a tail long enough for joining the 3 sts.
Slip the sts until reaching the center of the other motif (two hearts as one). Attach red and make another "heel" the same way but do not cut yarn after completing the 5 rows at tip. Slip half a row of sts onto a long circular until you reach the 3 sts on the other side. Join the sts into a ring and secure with a rubber band. Set aside these sts while you work one foot.

Foot
Join the 3-st strips at each side with three-needle bind-off (see page 11). The working yarn should be hanging loose and the knitting continues from that point. As you work the foot, change to dpn when the sts no longer fit around the circular. Now begin the foot where the yarn is attached. This is the beginning of the round and there is already a stitch there because of the join. First pick up and knit sts along the 5 rows that were knitted back and forth at the tip. Insert the needle through the loop and bring the yarn through (use a crochet hook instead if that is easier). Pick up about 3 sts at first and then knit over the unworked sts from the diagonal edge and all the way around until you again pick up and knit 4 sts – 52 sts total. Continue knitting around for approx 1½ – 2 in / 4 – 5 cm.

Toe
Count the number of sts. The toe is worked over a multiple of 6 sts. Decrease the extra sts on

the first rnd (*k11, k2tog; rep from * around) so the total is a multiple of 6 – 48 sts remain. Knit 2 rnds and then continue as explained for the toe shaping in the Basic Instructions (page 12). Cut yarn and draw end through remaining 8 sts; pull tight.

For the other foot, pick up and knit the same number of sts along the 5-row strip as for the first foot). Work foot and toe the same way.

Finishing

Weave in all ends securely on WS except for the cast-on tail. Make a red I-cord and a hanging loop at each side, beginning at one side. Graft the second hanging loop to beginning of I-cord edging. Weave in remaining ends. Wash and block the stocking (see page 11). For the model shown here, I made 4 small black tassels. I wrapped the tassels with red and embellished the wraps with black. The strand coming from the top of each tassel is about 1½ in / 4 cm long when twisted and folded double. Attach a little cord to each tassel and hide ends in tassel (see photo). Wash the tassels and shake out well. Attach 2 tassels at each side with a pewter button.

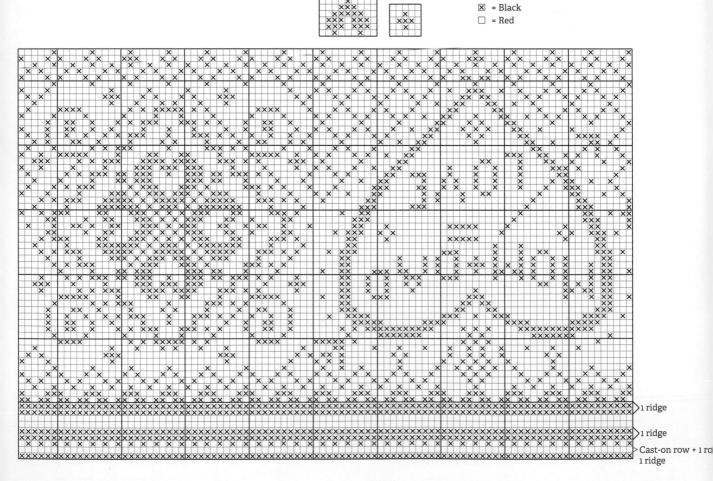

⊠ = Black
☐ = Red

1 ridge
1 ridge
Cast-on row + 1 ro
1 ridge

Heidi

Before you begin knitting, read the Basic Instructions for 3-ply Strikkegarn yarn (page 13), and Two-Color Stranded Knitting (page 10), paying particular attention to the advice about catching the floats on the wrong side. This design has five 3-color rounds.

Yarn

Rauma 3-ply Strikkegarn, 1 ball each: red 144, brown-black 110, green 145, yellow 131, white 101

Needles

U.S. sizes 2-3 and 4 / 3 and 3.5 mm

Instructions

With larger size needle and red, K-CO 60 sts (see page 10). Join, being careful not to twist cast-on row. Work around following the chart (next page). After completing charted rows, change to smaller needle and continue with red only for approx 1¼ in / 3 cm (knit 10 – 12 rnds).

Heel

Follow the Basic Instructions for the heel on page 13. This design has 1 center st. The heel is worked over 29 sts – 14 sts on each side of the center st. After decreasing 3 times on each side, work the heart motif using a long strand of black and intarsia technique (see small chart on next page). You can also embroider the heart on with duplicate stitch when the stocking is finished. Begin motif on a RS row.

Toe

Follow the Basic Instructions for the foot and toe on page 13. After decreasing 2 times + 1 rnd, attach black and make the zigzag motif (see chart on next page). On the next decrease rnd, k2tog between the points of the motif.

Finishing

Weave in all ends securely on WS except for the cast-on tail. With colors of your choice and larger needle, make an I-Cord edging and hanging loop along the top of the stocking. I made a green and red cord for this stocking. Graft the hanging loop to the beginning of the I-cord edging and weave in all remaining ends. Wash and block the stocking (see page 11).

Make a braid about 13¾ in / 35 cm long with 3 strands each red, black, and yellow. Divide the braid in two and twist white and green yarn around the ends with white in the center and green on each side. Gently wash the braids so they will be smoother. Fold each braid to double it and arrange the 4 little braids close together so they lay flat, one next to the other, and attach at the hanging loop.

For this stocking, we used an old Norwegian one-øring coin as a button. You can use a pewter button or a vintage button. We also made a little red tassel wrapped with green and black (above and below the green) for the toe.

Wash the tassel so it is plumped up. Twist the yarn at the top of the tassel for a cord about 1¼ in / 3 cm long and attach at the tip of the stocking toe. See photo.

⊠ = Black
☐ = Red
⊙ = Yellow
⊡ = White
◉ = Green

Toe

Heel

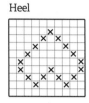

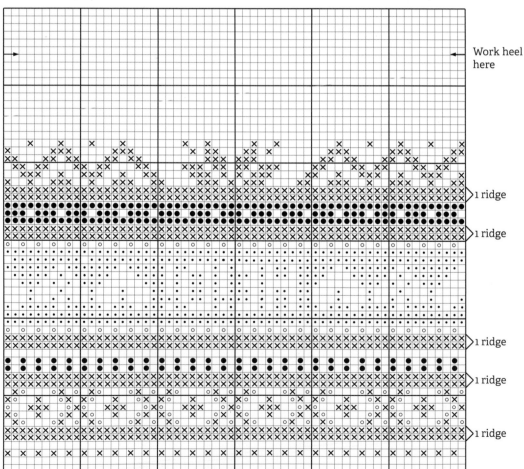

← Work heel here

⟩1 ridge

⟩1 ridge

⟩1 ridge

⟩1 ridge

⟩1 ridge

Christmas Baskets

Before you begin knitting, read the Basic Instructions for 3-ply Strikkegarn yarn (page 13), and Two-Color Stranded Knitting (page 10), paying particular attention to the advice about catching the floats on the wrong side. This design has seven 3-color rounds.

Yarn

Rauma 3-ply Strikkegarn, 1 ball each: dark red 128, bright red 124, white 101, brown-black 110, yellow 131

Needles

U.S. sizes 2-3 and 4 / 3 and 3.5 mm

Instructions

With smaller size needle and bright red, K-CO 60 sts (see page 10). Join, being careful not to twist cast-on row. Work following the chart (page 62) to the heel, changing to larger needle when you begin two-color patterning.

Heel

The bright red triangle closest to the center back is now the center st. Slip the 14 sts to the right of this point back onto left needle. Attach the center of a contrast color strand of yarn (about 1 yd / m long) and *knit 1, sl 1*; rep * to * until you have 29 sts. Slip the sts back to the point where you left the main color. This creates a "dot" row.

Knit until 1 st before the contrast yarn; turn, sl 1, purl back to the contrast yarn on the opposite side. Continue until there are 7 unworked sts on each side and 13 sts at the center. Knit 1 round over all the sts. Continue decreasing as explained in the Basic Instructions on page 13. When the heel is complete, slip the same 14 sts from the center st. Use the loose strand and work a "dot" row (k1 bright red, sl 1) on 29 sts. Slip sts back to the center st.

Foot

Knit around on the foot for approx 2¾ in / 7 cm or desired length (the toe will be about 2¾ in / 7 cm long. On the next rnd, work (k1 dark red, k1 bright red) around. Cut bright red and continue with dark red only. Knit 1 rnd with dark red.

Toe

Follow the Basic Instructions for the toe on page 13.

Finishing

Weave in all ends securely on WS except for the cast-on tail. Make an I-cord edging and hanging loop with dark red and larger needle. Graft the hanging loop to the beginning of the I-cord edging. Wash and block the stocking (see page 11). Make a little red pompom for the toe (see photo) and attach securely.

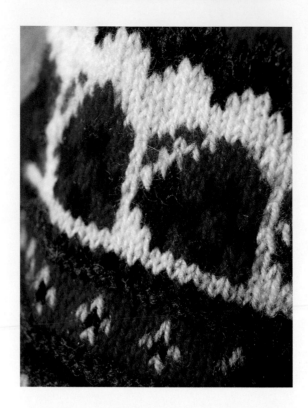

☐ = White
☑ = Dark Brown
■ = Black
☒ = Dark Red
⊡ = Red
⊙ = Yellow

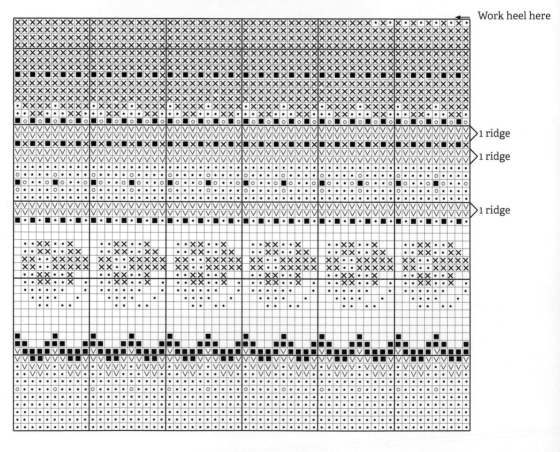

Work heel here

1 ridge
1 ridge
1 ridge

REINDEER AND SPRUCE TREES ▶

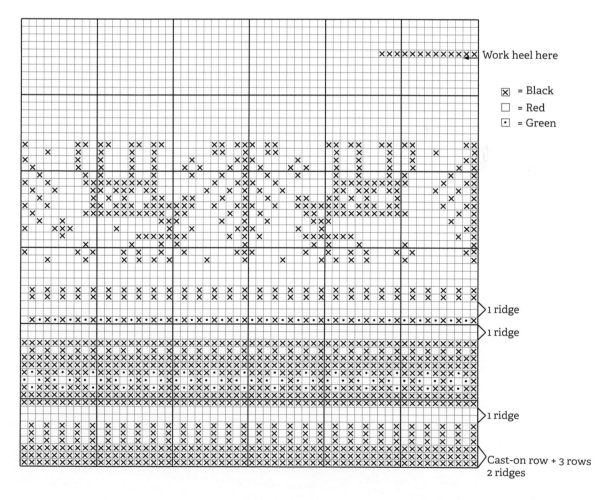

Work heel here

⊠ = Black
□ = Red
⊡ = Green

1 ridge

1 ridge

1 ridge

Cast-on row + 3 rows
2 ridges

Reindeer and Spruce Trees

Before you begin knitting, read the Basic Instructions for 3-ply Strikkegarn yarn (page 13), and Two-Color Stranded Knitting (page 10), paying particular attention to the advice about catching the floats on the wrong side. This design has one 3-color round.

Yarn
Rauma 3-ply Strikkegarn, 1 ball each: red 144, brown-black 110, green 145

Needles
U.S. sizes 2-3 and 4 / 3 and 3.5 mm

Instructions
With larger size needle and black, K-CO 60 sts (see page 10). Join, being careful not to twist cast-on row. Work following the chart (page 63) to the heel, changing to smaller needle after finishing the reindeer. The black yarn is used for the center back st on every other rnd down to the heel. Knit around until the stocking measures approx 8 in / 20 cm. Cut black.

Heel
See Basic Instructions for the short-row heel on page 13. Slip 16 sts beginning at center back and then work 32 sts with black using a strand approx 27½ in / 70 cm long. Slip 16 sts back onto left needle. Work the short-row heel as explained on page 13 in the Basic Instructions but *do not knit 3 complete rnds*. End at center back and do not cut yarn.
Slip the sts back to where the black strand is hanging on the right side. Knit to the other side of the heel – 32 sts. Slip the sts until again at the center back, where the red yarn is attached.

Foot
Attach a new strand of black yarn about 2 yd / m long. Knit the last st on every other rnd with black. Make sure that you twist the yarns when changing colors: Hold the red yarn to the left, bring the black around it and knit 1 st; hold this yarn at left and continue with red.
Continue the same way for 2¾ – 3½ in / 7 – 9 cm. The toe will add another 2¾ in / 7 cm to the total foot length. Knit 1 rnd with black and then 1 rnd with red before beginning toe shaping. Cut black.

Toe
Work as described in the Basic Instructions on page 13.

Finishing
Weave in all ends securely on WS except for the cast-on tail. Make an I-cord edging and hanging loop with green and larger needle. Graft hanging loop to beginning of I-cord edging. Wash and block the stocking (see page 11).
This stocking has a little red and green rosette at the hanging loop. Make a 3-part cord (see explanation in "Snowmen" on page 42). Make a black tassel wrapped with green yarn for the longest cord. Wash the tassel and shake it out well so it will hang smoothly. I found some tiny cowbells to attach to the two short cords. Sleigh bells or several tassels will also work well (see photo).

Christmas Baskets and Lice

Before you begin knitting, read the Basic Instructions for 3-ply Strikkegarn yarn (page 13), and Two-Color Stranded Knitting (page 10), paying particular attention to the advice about catching the floats on the wrong side.

You can use small amounts of leftover yarns for this stocking. You are sure to find several colors that will work together in your yarn basket. For example, you can use assorted colors for the lice. The Christmas baskets should be red but they will also look very nice in any shade of green.

Yarn

Rauma 3-ply Strikkegarn, 1 ball each: red 124, rust red 144, dark red 180, yellow 131, pink 173

Needles

U.S. sizes 2-3 and 4 / 3 and 3.5 mm

Instructions

With larger size needle and red, K-CO 60 sts (see page 10). Join, being careful not to twist cast-on row. Work following the chart (page 68) to the heel, changing to smaller needle when you begin the lice (small dots of color) pattern. Let the dark red strand hang below the main panel at the top because it will be used for the first "lice" round. The stocking shown here has 9 lice rows above the heel and 7 afterwards. Because there are so many lice colors, cut and weave in the ends when finishing the stocking.

Heel

Work the heel with the same color as for the zigzag panel below the baskets. Work the heel over 29 sts with 14 sts on each side of a center st. Work over all the sts plus 1 st on each side, for a total of 31 heel sts. Continue the heel shaping until there are once again 14 sts on each side of the center st. Leave the yarn hanging loose to use in the next lice round.

Toe

The last pattern panel is worked before the toe shaping begins. Begin the zigzag stripe with the same color as the heel and work the toe itself with dark red. Knit 1 rnd before the first decrease rnd for the toe. Work toe as described in the Basic Instructions on page 13.

Finishing

Weave in all ends securely on WS except for the cast-on tail. With larger needle, make an I-cord edging and hanging loop with the same red as for the heel. Graft hanging loop to beginning of I-cord edging. Wash and block the stocking (see page 11).

The stocking can be embellished with some tassels and this model has 5 tassels in 5 different colors. Each tassel is wrapped with a contrast color. Trim each tassel into a small point. Make a red cord with doubled yarn 15¾ – 19¾ in / 40 – 50 cm long. Hold it in your right hand and pull out 6 in / 15 cm to make a short cord; hold the cord securely in your right hand together with the end of the cord. Make 5 little cords one after the other and hold onto them well.

Twist around all the little cords with red yarn to make 1 tassel at the top. Attach each of the 5 tassels to its own small cord. Wash gently the tassels so they'll hang more smoothly. Attach the bundle to the stocking at the hanging loop using the color that best matches the stripe at the top. See photo on page 68.

◄ CHRISTMAS BASKETS AND LICE

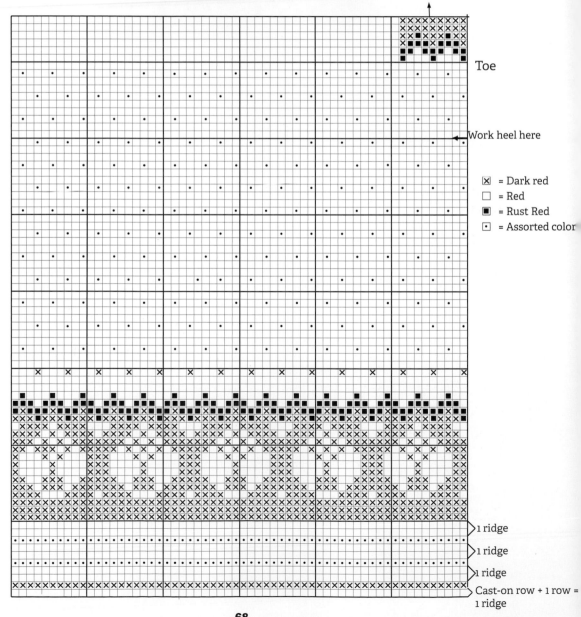

Toe

Work heel here

☒ = Dark red
☐ = Red
■ = Rust Red
⊡ = Assorted color

1 ridge
1 ridge
1 ridge
Cast-on row + 1 row = 1 ridge

BUTTER CHURN ROSE ▶

+ 1 repeat

↑

← Work heel here

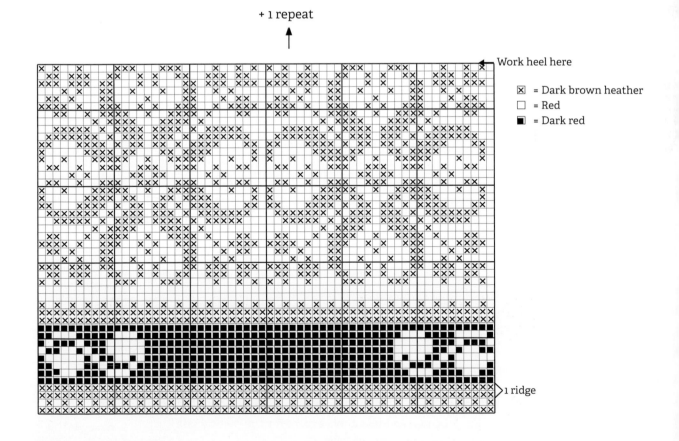

⊠ = Dark brown heather
☐ = Red
■ = Dark red

〉1 ridge

Butter Churn Rose
Motif from Selbu

The Butter Churn rose pattern could be found as a wreath embossed on the end of the rod on a butter churn.
The motif on the top panel is a "separator hook."

Before you begin knitting, read the Basic Instructions for 3-ply Strikkegarn yarn (page 13), and Two-Color Stranded Knitting (page 10), paying particular attention to the advice about catching the floats on the wrong side.

Yarn
Rauma 3-ply Strikkegarn, 1 ball each: red 124, brown heather 164, dark red 128

Needles
U.S. sizes 2-3 and 4 / 3 and 3.5 mm

Instructions
With larger size needle and brown, K-CO 60 sts (see cast-on instructions, page 10). Join, being careful not to twist cast-on row. Work following the chart (page 69) to the heel. After completing the charted rows, knit 1 rnd with red before working heel.

Heel
Change to smaller needle. Work the heel over 29 sts with 7 sts on each side of the center st and 15 sts at the center. The heel is worked in stripes: 2 rows brown, 2 rows dark red, 2 rows red. The third red stripe is worked around over all the sts (2 rnds). Continue with the rest of the heel in stripes working the last 2 rows with 31 sts (= increase 1 st at each side).

Foot
Change back to larger needle. Work 1 pattern repeat and then knit 1 rnd with red. Change to smaller needle for toe.

Toe
The first decrease rnd is worked with red and worked as described in the Basic Instructions on page 13. Work in stripes as for the heel.

Finishing
Weave in all ends securely on WS except for the cast-on tail. Turn the stocking inside out and, with larger needle, make a dark red I-cord for the edge and hanging loop. Graft the hanging loop to the beginning of the I-cord edging. Wash and block the stocking (see page 11).

Two Hearts

Before you begin knitting, read the Basic Instructions for 3-ply Strikkegarn yarn (page 13), and Two-Color Stranded Knitting (page 10), paying particular attention to the advice about catching the floats on the wrong side. This design has three 3-color rounds.

Yarn
Rauma 3-ply Strikkegarn, 1 ball each: dark green 123, red 144, green 145

Needles
U.S. sizes 2-3 and 4 / 3 and 3.5 mm

Instructions
With larger size needle and green, K-CO 60 sts (see page 10). Join, being careful not to twist cast-on row. Work following the chart (page 74) to the heel. Change to smaller needle.

Heel
Work the short-row heel as described in the Basic Instructions on page 13.

Foot and Toe
Work as described in the Basic Instructions on page 13. After the first decrease rnd for the toe, knit 1 rnd, and then work the small panel (see chart). Complete toe following Basic Instructions.

Finishing
Weave in all ends securely on WS except for the cast-on tail. Turn the stocking inside out and, with larger needle, make a red I-cord for the edge and hanging loop. Graft the hanging loop to the beginning of the I-cord edging. Wash and block the stocking (see page 11).

◄ TWO HEARTS

☒ = Red

☐ = Dark green

⊡ = Green

Toe

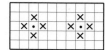

Work heel here →

← Work here

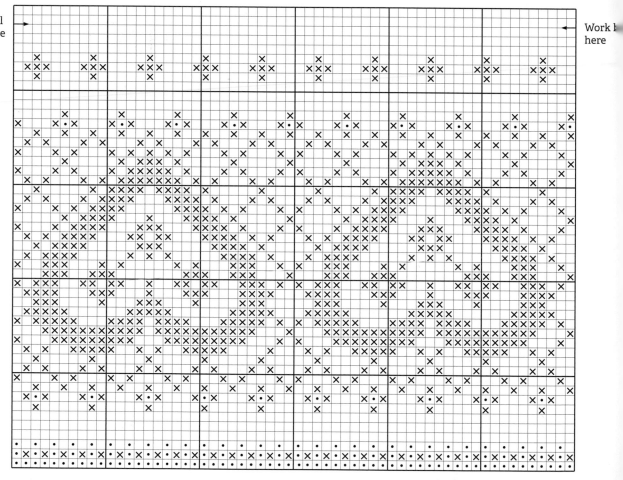

74

CHRISTMAS ROSES 1 AND 2 ▶

☒ = Dark green
☐ = Red
■ = Green

☒ = Pale red
☐ = Terra cotta red
■ = Black
• = Yellow

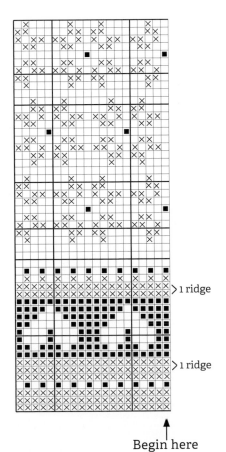

> 1 ridge

> 1 ridge

Begin here

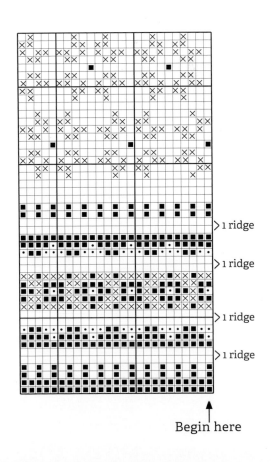

> 1 ridge

> 1 ridge

> 1 ridge

> 1 ridge

Begin here

75

Christmas Roses 1 and 2

Before you begin knitting, read the Basic Instructions for 3-ply Strikkegarn yarn (page 13), and Two-Color Stranded Knitting (page 10), paying particular attention to the advice about catching the floats on the wrong side. Christmas Roses 2 has one 3-color round.

Yarn

Rauma 3-ply Strikkegarn, 1 ball each color:
Christmas Roses 1: dark green 15/61, red 174, green 145
Christmas Roses 2: brown-black 110, terra cotta red 127, pale red 157, yellow 131

Needles

U.S. sizes 2-3 and 4 / 3 and 3.5 mm

Instructions

With larger size needle and dark green or black, K-CO 60 sts (see page 10). Join, being careful not to twist cast-on row. Work following chart 1 or 2 (page 75) to the heel. Christmas Roses 1 has 3 rows of roses and Christmas Roses 2 has 2. After the heel, each version has 2 rows of roses. **Note:** that chart 2 has one 3-color round. Follow the chart on page 75 for the rose pattern.

Heel

Because of the design, the heel has 1 center st.

Work the heel over 29 sts. Change to smaller needle and begin after the last pattern row. Work the center st + 14 sts; turn, sl 1 purlwise, p29. Continue the heel as described in the Basic Instructions (page 13). When there are 7 unworked sts at each side of the heel and 15 sts at center back, work over all the unworked sts: Knit the center st + 15 sts; turn, purl back over 31 sts; turn. Work 1 rnd and then continue shaping the heel.

Foot and Toe

After the heel is complete, change to larger needle and work 2 repeats of the rose motif. Change to smaller needle and knit 3 rnds. Cut black and pale red. Work toe as described in the Basic Instructions on page 13.

Finishing

Weave in all ends securely on WS except for the cast-on tail. Use the main color to make an I-cord for the edge and hanging loop. For Christmas Roses 2, you can make a 2-color I-cord using the same colors as for the roses. Graft the hanging loop to the beginning of the I-cord edging. Wash and block the stocking (see page 11). Christmas Roses 1 is embellished with a small red/green rosette and a sleigh bell attached at the hanging loop (see photo on page 75).

Heart Stocking

Before you begin knitting, read the Basic Instructions for 3-ply Strikkegarn yarn (page 13), and Two-Color Stranded Knitting (page 10), paying particular attention to the advice about catching the floats on the wrong side.

You can use small amounts of yarn you have on hand for this stocking. I used 3 shades of red for my version but, of course, you can choose whatever colors you like.

Yarn

Rauma 3-ply Strikkegarn, 1 ball each: eggplant 180, bright red 124, pink 173

Needles

U.S. sizes 2-3 and 4 / 3 and 3.5 mm

Instructions

With larger size needle and eggplant, K-CO 60 sts (see page 10). Join, being careful not to twist cast-on row. Work following chart on page 80 to the heel.

Heel

Cut bright red and pink and work heel with eggplant only. Change to smaller needle. Because of the design, the heel has 1 center st at center back. Work the heel over 29 sts = 14 sts on each side of the center back st. See Basic Instructions on page 13 for details on shaping the heel but use the number of sts specified here. When there are 7 unworked sts at each side of the heel and 15 sts at center back, work over all the unworked sts: Knit the center st + 15 sts; turn, purl back over 31 sts; turn. Work the rest of the heel with eggplant and then return to the charted pattern.

Foot and Toe

Change to larger needle. Attach all 3 colors at center back of sock and continue charted pattern. After completing charted rows, cut bright red and pink and change to smaller needle. Work toe as described in the Basic Instructions on page 13.

Finishing

Weave in all ends securely on WS except for the cast-on tail. With larger needle and bright red, make an I-cord for the edge and hanging loop. Graft the hanging loop to the beginning of the I-cord edging. Wash and block the stocking (see page 11).

◄ HEART STOCKING

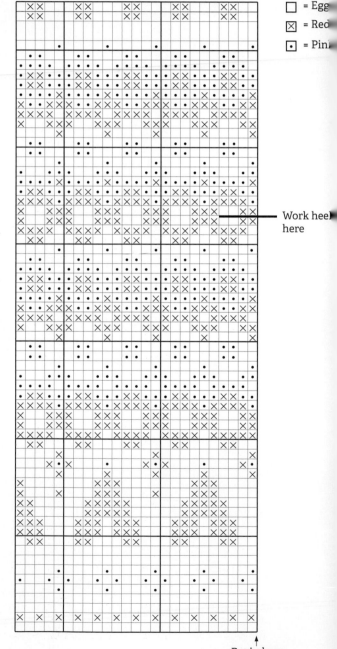

= Egg

= Red

= Pin

Work heel here

Begin here

TEDDY BEAR ▶

Continue with single color

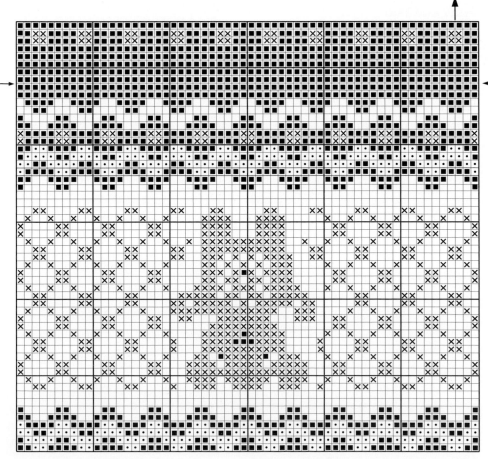

← Work heel here

■ = Red
□ = Ochre yellow
☒ = Yellow
⋅ = Orange

Teddy Bear

Before you begin knitting, read the Basic Instructions for 3-ply Strikkegarn yarn (page 13), and Two-Color Stranded Knitting (page 10), paying particular attention to the advice about catching the floats on the wrong side.

Yarn
Rauma 3-ply Strikkegarn, 1 ball each: red 144, ochre yellow 146, yellow 131, orange 177

Needles
U.S. sizes 2-3 and 4 / 3 and 3.5 mm

Instructions
With larger size needle and red, K-CO 60 sts (see page 10). Join, being careful not to twist cast-on row. Work following chart on page 81) to the heel (note that there are 2 red rounds before the heel begins). You can knit in the snout and eyes or embroider them later with duplicate stitch.

Heel and Foot
Change to smaller needle for the heel and foot. Work the heel with red. Work heel and foot
as described in the Basic Instructions on page 13.

Toe
Work as described in the Basic Instructions on page 13 but continue decreasing with k2tog until 4 sts remain. With the remaining 4 sts, make an I-cord about 5 rows long. Now increase with M1 between every st (= 8 sts) and work a few more rows. Knit 1 rnd. Increase on alternate rounds with one st more between increases on each increase round until there are 18 sts total – the piece will look like a little funnel or a mini-elf cap. Turn the work inside out and loosely BO knitwise on the WS.

Finishing
Weave in all ends securely on WS except for the cast-on tail. Turn the stocking inside out and, with larger needle and two colors, make an I-cord for the edge and hanging loop. Graft the hanging loop to the beginning of the I-cord edging. Wash and block the stocking (see page 11).
Make a firm pompom to attach to the tip of the toe on the little "elf cap." Wash the pompom and shake out well. Trim the pompom so it is even all around. After attaching the pompom to the inside of the funnel, stitch around the edges so that the whole section hangs nicely.

Elf Cap

Before you begin knitting, read the section on Two-Color Stranded Knitting (page 10), paying particular attention to the advice about catching the floats on the wrong side. This design has one 3-color round.

Yarn
Rauma 3-ply Strikkegarn, 1 ball each: red 174, white 101, brown-black 110, green 145, yellow 131
Rauma 2-ply Gammelserie is used for the facing: red and black

Needles
U.S. sizes 1-2, 2-3, and 4 / 2.5, 3 and 3.5 mm

Note: The cap is a bit large, so do not knit loosely. Change to smaller needles if necessary.

Instructions
With smallest needle and 2-ply Gammelserie yarn, K-CO 126 sts (see page 10). This cast-on method is more elastic. Join, being careful not to twist cast-on row and knit around for approx 4 in / 10 cm. The facing can be single color or alternately knit with 2 rnds each of red and black Gammelserie yarn; end with 2 rnds red.
Change to 3-ply Strikkegarn and needles U.S. 2-3 / 3 mm. The next round is an eyelet foldline: (yo, k2tog) around. Turn work and knit back = 1 garter ridge. Continue, working charted pattern on page 86. Change to largest needle when beginning the main pattern and change to medium size needle when two-color knitting is complete. You can knit the black eyes with short strands of yarn for each figure or embroider on the black eyes later with duplicate stitch. Finish with 2 rnds red.
On the next rnd, decrease 6 sts evenly spaced around: (K19, k2tog) around. Knit 6 rnds.
Now begin decreasing at 4 points evenly spaced around. Place a marker on each side of 3 sts centered at these 4 places. There should be 27 sts between each set of 3 marked sts. Begin decreasing at center back. Decrease with ssk before each group of 3 marked sts and k2tog after the marked sts.

Note: When decreasing with ssk, sl 1 knitwise, sl 1 knitwise, insert left needle from left to right (the tip of the left needle will be in front of the right needle) into the 2 sts on right needle and knit the 2 sts together. This will make the sts snug and the pairs of decreases will be mirror image. Decrease with 6 rnds between each decrease rnd 3 times. Now decrease every 6th rnd. When 16 sts remain, knit 5 rnds and then k2tog around until 8 sts remain. Cut yarn and pull through remaining sts; pull snug.

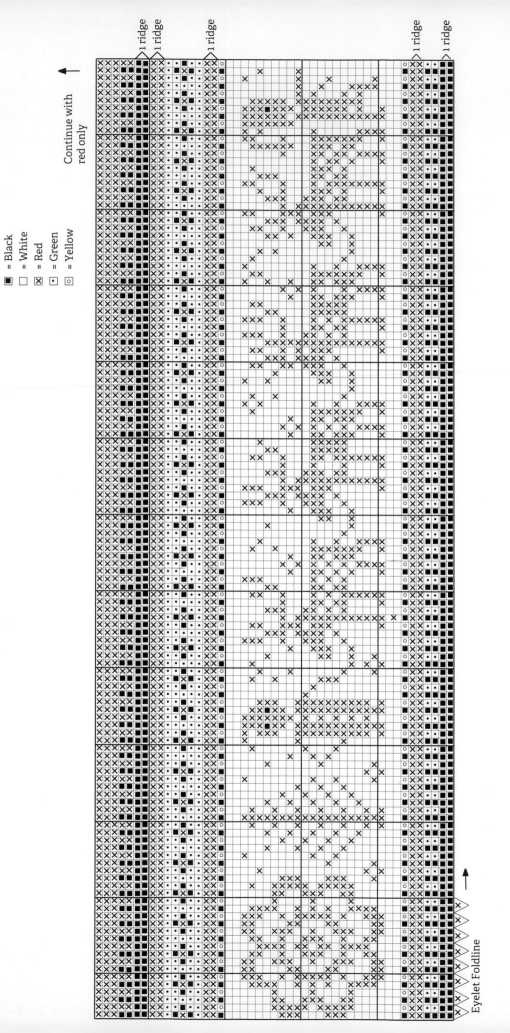

= Black
= White
= Red
= Green
= Yellow

Continue with
red only

1 ridge 1 ridge 1 ridge 1 ridge 1 ridge

Eyelet Foldline

ELF CAP

Finishing

Weave in all ends securely on WS. If the facing is too short, you can easily pick up and knit sts from the cast-on row and add a few more rounds. In this case, BO elastically: K2tog, *slip st back to left needle, k2tog; rep from * around. Sew down lining along a garter stitch ridge of the main pattern. Sew down the lining on WS using finer, 2-ply Gammelserie yarn, with 1 sewn stitch in each knit stitch. Wash and block the cap (see page 11).

You can make a large tassel or pompom for the tip of the cap, either a really thick ball or a long tassel. You can decorate the tassel by winding on stripes of yarn and securing it closely to the cap or letting the tassel hang freely.

For the cap shown here, we made a little red and black pompom attached to a short cord. You can make a decorated pompom on a long cord instead: twist a cord about 19¾ in / 50 cm long. Double the cord and let twist together. Bind into a circle. The pompom is wound around your hand with a little black first and then a lot of red. Secure at the center and clip open. Wrap three circles around the outspread pompom so that the knot comes below, inside the "head" of the pompom. Sew it here and tie a knot on the doubled cord. It might be a little thick so use a needle to help pull it through.

Gather all the loose yarn strands together and twist together with black. Decorate above and below the black with strands of other colors, such as yellow and green. You can then embellish the green strands with small stitches (see photos of similar embellishments on pages 33 and 55). Wash the pompom carefully and shake it into shape so it will be plumper. Attach cord securely to the tip of the cap.

Mittens

Before you begin knitting, read the section on Two-Color Stranded Knitting (page 10), paying particular attention to the advice about catching the floats on the wrong side.

Yarn

Rauma 3-ply Strikkegarn, 1 ball each: red 174, white 101, brown-black 110

Needles

Set of 4 or 5 dpn U.S. sizes 1-2, 2-3, and 4 / 2.5, 3 and 3.5 mm

Instructions

A black stripe is worked up each side of the mitten. Cut a length of black yarn about 47¼ in / 120 cm long for each side (and about 23¾ in / 60 cm long for the thumb) and add in on the first round after the border. Twist around the stitch on every round up the hand. At first it will seem fiddly working this way but actually it is a good method for catching the strands. Hold the yarn to the left and bring the black strand up, to the left first, and then pull it under and out rightwards after every stitch. You can make the stripe white if you prefer.

For a more elastic cast-on row, K-CO 44 sts with black and smallest size dpn; join being careful not to twist cast-on row. Work in stockinette for 8 rnds with. Change to medium size needles and knit 6 rnds. On the next rnd, increase 4 sts evenly spaced around. Change to red and make the eyelet foldine: (yo, k2tog) around.

Cuff

Knit the cuff border pattern first. Cut the green and yellow yarn; add the approx 47¼ in / 120 cm long strand of black. Continue working charted pattern on page 91. It will be easiest if you arrange the stitches so that the black is the next-to-last-stitch on the needle. There are two charts for the palm so you can choose the one you like. There is 1 rnd more of white so you should begin with the back of the hand and then work the palm.

Hand

Change to largest needles when the main pattern begins.

When you reach the dark line on the chart for the thumbhole, place the 12 sts for the thumb on a stitch holder or waste yarn. On the next rnd, cast on 12 new sts. One method for casting on is to make a half-hitch (loop) on the left hand and place this loop in on the right needle. The new stitches just cast on should match the colors shown on the chart. Throughout, twist the 2 colors around each other the same way. Continue working charted pattern to top shaping.

Top Shaping

There should be 5 sts on each side of the mitten and these 5 sts continue as is to the tip of the mitten. Decreases are made after/before this edge panel. The first decrease is an ssk (see Abbreviations on page 10). K2tog on the opposite side of the mitten front. Decrease the same way on the palm and throughout. Because there will be less white in the pattern and long floats at the sides, I recommend that you catch the black strands in the two other colors.

When 12 sts remain, decrease on one side only. There should only be the 10 side sts left at the end.

To make a rounded top of the mitten, you can join these sts with three-needle bind-off worked from the inside. Cut yarn leaving a tail about 8 in / 20 cm long. Slip the remaining sts onto waste yarn (or 5-5 onto two locking ring markers). Holding the sts/yarn securely, turn the mitten inside out. Divide the sts 5-5 onto 2 dpn and hold the needles parallel. The stitches can now be joined with three-

Note: Chart on page 91 has 2013 on it.

needle bind-off: insert the right needle in the first st on the front needle, then into the first st on the back needle, catch the red yarn and bring through both stitches. Knit the next st the same way. Pass the first st over the second (bind off), knit the next st with black. BO. Knit the last two sts with red.

Thumb

Place the 12 thumb sts on a dpn. Pick up and knit sts around the thumb-hole following the chart on page 91. On the side facing the front of the thumb, pick up 1 black st in the black stripe. Attach a new strand of black so you can work the black stripe at each side of the thumb as for the hand. Work thumb following the chart. Shape top as described for top of hand. When 8 sts remain, cut yarn and draw end through remaining sts.

Finishing

Weave in all ends securely on WS and sew down the facing. Remove one ply from the yarn so it will be a bit finer and sew with small, fine stitches, with one sewn st into each knit stitch.

MITTENS

= Black
= Red
= White
= Green
= Yellow

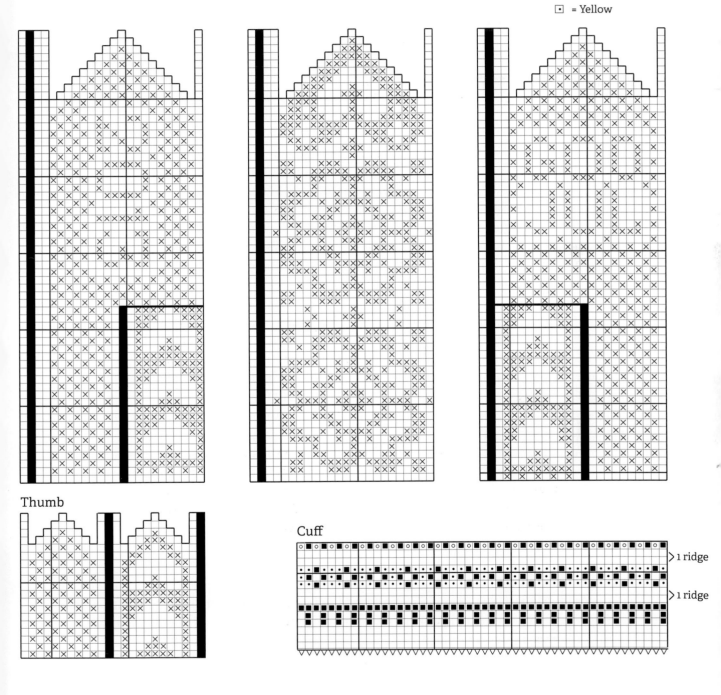

Thumb

Cuff

> 1 ridge

> 1 ridge

Leggings

Yarn
Rauma 3-ply Strikkegarn, 1 ball each: red 174, brown-black 110, green 145, yellow 131

Needles
U.S. sizes 2-3, and 4 / 3 and 3.5 mm

Instructions
The motif on the front of each legging is worked in intarsia as you knit in the round. This technique can be fun but perhaps a little complicated.

There is one 3-color round.

With smaller needle and black, K-CO 52 sts; do not join. Work back and forth in k2, p2 ribbing for approx 7 – 8 rows. Knit the next row, increasing 4 sts evenly spaced across and then knit back = 1 garter ridge.

Now join to work in the round and change to larger size needle. Work following the bottom chart on page 95 and then continue with red. *At the same time*, about every 2 in / 5 cm, increase 2 sts at the center back a total of 4 times. The leggings should be approx 12¼ in / 31 cm around at the top. If they are too small, increase every 1½ in / 4 cm 5 times.

When the piece measures approx 6¾ in / 17 cm long, begin the dancing figure motif. Place a marker at the center front.

Intarsia knitting in the round, man's figure
Rnd 1: Attach black and knit the 2 pattern sts on the chart and then continue around with red.
Rnd 2: Hold the red strand to the left and k1 with black; move the black strand to the left and continue around with red.
Rnd 3: Work as set, twisting colors around each other when changing.
Rnd 4: Knit with red to the motif. Now follow the pattern carefully, knitting the red sts and slipping the sts that would be knit with black. Knit with red until 1 st past the motif and turn. Work back in pattern, purling the black sts (those slipped on previous row) and slipping the red sts. Turn work again and work back to the red yarn. Continue around. Always twist the yarns around each other 1 st past the pattern to avoid a hole where the colors change.
Rnd 5: Work to pattern, k1 black, twist yarns, continue. Twist strands together often.

When you know that the yarn on the next round should begin a little further towards the left, I recommend that you work a couple of sts past the previous turn, and twist yarns. This is especially important when working the figure's arms.

Note: Don't forget the increases at the center back as you work the figure.

Intarsia knitting in the round, woman's figure
Rnd 1: K2. Continue with 2 red, twist yarns, k2 red, twist yarns. Continue around.
Continue the same way as for the man's figure and don't forget to twist the yarns around each other 1 st past the pattern.

Note: Don't forget the increases at the center back as you work the figure.

When the figure is complete, work 3 rnds in red and then continue with the charted pattern at top of page 95. Count out from the center stitch to determine where the panel begins.

I made an eyelet rnd for the foldline of my leggings. Change to black and work eyelet rnd: (k2tog, yo) around. Change to smaller size

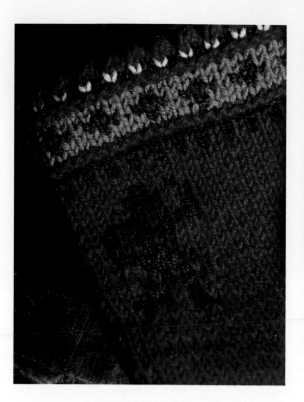

needle and continue with the facing. After 2 rnds, decrease 4 sts evenly spaced around. Knit 11 rnds with black and then bind off loosely (see page 11).

Alternately, you can make a black garter ridge (knit 1 rnd, purl 1 rnd) for the foldline and then work facing as above.

Finishing

If the figure needs some freshening up to look nice, you can easily dampen the piece and tug at it here and there. Split a length of yarn and use the thinnest strand to catch any stray loops on the back.

Weave in the remaining ends securely on the WS. Sew down the facing, using 2 strands of the 3-ply yarn for finer stitching. Sew down with small tight stitches, with one sewn st in every knit st.

Seam the ribbing. Carefully steam press the leggings so that the figures are completely flat (see photo).

LEGGINGS

Foldline

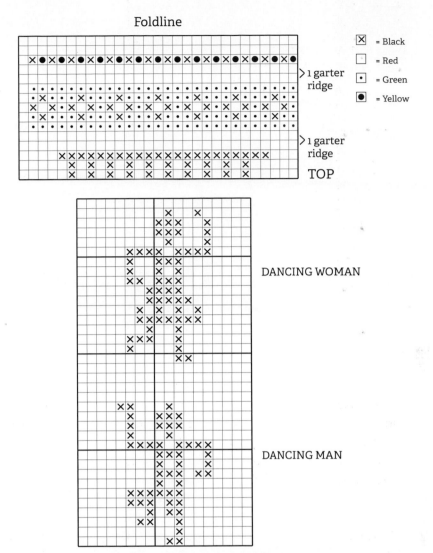

> 1 garter ridge

> 1 garter ridge

TOP

- ☒ = Black
- ☐ = Red
- ⊡ = Green
- ⬤ = Yellow

DANCING WOMAN

DANCING MAN

The single-color section measures 6¾ in / 17 cm

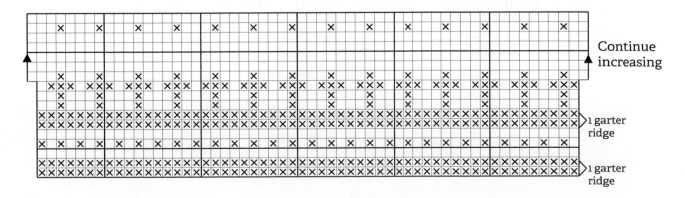

Continue increasing

> 1 garter ridge

> 1 garter ridge